Coming to and Living in Germany

Heike Wolf

Table of Contents

I. Introduction

The trend to spend several years – or maybe even the rest of one's life – in a foreign country by now is an integral part of many people's lives. The reasons for leaving one's home country are manifold; often the first longer stay abroad takes place during university years, as more and more students have realized the importance of such stays abroad. During career life many companies encourage or even demand international flexibility of their employees and especially managers or future managers welcome the chance of gaining business experience in other countries and cultures as so-called expatriates, often taking their spouses and children with them. Expatriate communities are growing rapidly all over the world as well as in the internet, often forming their own "expat culture" as they bring together people of all nationalities and the culture of the current host country. Some people even start "expat careers", moving from one country to the other, without ever returning to their home country to live. Never before has the access to other countries and other cultures been as easy as in today's times of globalization, and most expats (in this book this term will be used for all persons who are living or have lived in a foreign country for a longer time) consider living in another country an important and rewarding experience. However, living in a foreign country of course is also a great challenge and can confront expats with certain problems, usually resulting from being unfamiliar with the host country's culture, customs and language. "Culture shock" is a term often used to describe this situation and, indeed, it can be a shock to be suddenly confronted with a completely different lifestyle. Generally, it can be said that thorough information about the host country and its customs can prevent or minimize a culture shock considerably and fortunately the internet as well as several books about life as an expat offer more and more detailed information about most countries.

I am German and worked in expatriate management for several years. Currently I am working as an intercultural trainer (www.wolfintercultural.com) and writing an intercultural blog.

Both in my work and in my private life I have met many expats and consider this a rewarding experience. I myself am also lucky to boast a relatively international family background, with a mother who grew up in the UK and a father who spent his youth in Belgium. With family members in Germany, the UK, Spain and Belgium, I have always had a special affinity for different countries and foreign languages. I had the opportunity of experiencing the life of an expat student, when I did my LL.M. (Master of Laws) degree in the United States, where I worked and lived for a while after I finished my studies. In the course of the LL.M. program, which was entirely international, I met many wonderful people from all over the world. I think it was there that I initially experienced the meaning of cultural differences and culture shock first-hand. Since then, this subject has fascinated me to a great extent.

This book will give you a picture of expat life in Germany. It is based on several questionnaires filled out by non-Germans who have lived in Germany for six months or longer. Their reasons for coming to live here are miscellaneous; many are accompanying spouses. They come from various countries and have made all kinds of experiences, which they kindly shared with me by answering the questionnaires. They also offered helpful advice on how to overcome culture shock, make German friends or how to deal with the authorities as well as handling daily tasks such as grocery shopping or finding a doctor. It is hands-on advice from people who have experienced living in Germany as expats. I would very much like to thank those who took the time and effort to fill out the questionnaires and also to give me valuable tips and information for this project. They shared a lot of useful knowledge that will make moving to Germany for future expats much easier. If you wish to contribute to this collection of knowledge and experiences, you are very welcome to share your thoughts on expat life by email (hwolf@wolfintercultural.com) or ask me for a questionnaire to fill out.

The main part of the book is therefore dedicated to the stories and experiences of the contributing expats. Some of the respondents to my questionnaire asked me not to mention their names and of course I respect this, therefore names will not always be given.

I added useful background information and an occasional German viewpoint and have also included links and literature tips in order to make this book an all-round useful information tool for you.

II. Preparation and Move

As mentioned in the introduction, a thorough knowledge of what to expect in the host country can help to minimize culture shock, and as everything strange and unfamiliar is always more fear-inducing than things that are better known, this book can also help overcome any anxieties you might have about undertaking the move abroad. If you know or at least can estimate what awaits you in your new temporary home country, you will be better equipped to overcome any difficulties and obstacles you might be confronted with. Surprisingly, hardly anyone who filled out the questionnaires mentioned that having looked at any books or websites for information, even though this is an easy and recommendable way of preparing for your stay abroad.

Apart from getting information about German culture, food or the living circumstances in your new home location, you should not neglect informing yourself about immigration laws, health care, the validity of your driver's license and other bureaucratic matters in order to avoid unpleasant surprises. There are many ways of acquiring information, and with some time and effort you can easily be well prepared for your move to and your stay in Germany. You should start your information search as soon as you know of your move to Germany (or even earlier, if you are still reflecting on the thought of moving, to find out whether it is a viable option for you).

You should also find out what tourist attractions Germany, in general, and your new home location, in particular, has to offer. If you discover things of interest in anticipation of your move, it will make the transition easier for you, as you then have something to look forward to. Many of the respondents to my questionnaire pointed out how much they enjoyed the numerous historical sights, such as the castles or old towns and cities as well as the diverse nature, from the plains in the north to the Alpes in Southern Germany. Expats from large countries like Canada, the US or Australia also appreciated Germany being so close to many other European countries, making it easy to discover those countries on weekend trips or short vacations.

Following, you will find several suggestions for books and websites I personally found informative and helpful. This is not a complete list of all useful sources, of course, but it might serve you as a first guideline.

1. Books

There are some helpful books describing life in Germany or about expat life in general. Of course, they vary in quality, so it is always a good idea to know what exactly you want to find out. If you are an experienced expat, you won't necessarily need books about how to adjust to the expat situation or how to overcome culture shock, you'd want to look for more specific information about Germany.

a. General Expat Books

* *The Expert Expat, Melissa Brayer Hess and Patricia Linderman*
  "The Expert Expat" is a book for expats that covers many practical topics, as well as accounts from expats. The books aims to guide you through the whole experience, starting with "how to tell the kids" and preparing the move and also giving tips on returning home. The authors have been expatriates themselves for many years. Especially recommendable is the chapter on helping children to adjust to the new situation.

* *Survival Kit for Overseas Living, L. Robert Kohls*
  The Survival Kit for Overseas Living is by now a classic of expat literature. First published in 1979 and with regular updates until today, this well-written book concentrates on the aspects of cultural differences and culture shock that accompany every international move. Its main target group is American expats. There are many comparisons with the American culture, but it is still useful to expats from any other countries, as the included information gives a valuable and interesting background about how cultures work and how expats can adjust to difficulties.

- *Homeward Bound : A Spouse's Guide to Repatriation, Robin Pascoe*
  This book touches a so-far somewhat neglected problem – the fact that moving back home after a stay in another country is not free of difficulties. These difficulties can be even harder to deal with as nobody expects them, because after all, one is returning home. However, culture shock can also occur when you come back home, it is then called reverse culture shock or re-entry shock. The target group is mainly accompanying spouses who face quite other difficulties upon returning home than their partners, and who, as mentioned before, belong to a group that is still highly neglected in the planning and executing of international work assignments. The book – unfortunately a bit dated by now – describes experiences you are likely to have and how to deal with them.

- *Diplomatic Baggage – The Adventures of a Trailing Spouse, Brigid Keenan*
  A first-hand account of a woman who spent thirty years living all around the world as a diplomat's wife. The writing style is witty and here you can read about life in really exotic countries. It's not a book with practical advice on expat life, but a readable true tale.

b. **Books about Living in Germany**

- *When in Germany, do as the Germans do, Hyde Flippo*
  This book is mainly for tourists traveling to Germany and offers a quick introduction to German culture. It is just as useful to expats coming to live in Germany. The book consists of several articles covering all kinds of aspects relating to Germany, from history, food and politics to entertainment. You can even test your knowledge with multiple-choice questions. However, when reading the book, remember that not all German areas are alike and that you get a somewhat light version of cultural aspects. It is definitely entertaining and a good start if you want to know more about your new home country, especially as you will get to read some unusual and interesting facts that are not generally covered in introductory books about Germany.

- *Germany: memories of a nation, Neil MacGregor*
  This is one of my personal favourites, not just with regard to the expat experience, but in general. The book is based on an exhibition in the British Museum and offers in-depth and entertaining information about German history and how it shaped German culture. Even I as a German history buff learned quite a lot from this book, and if you want to really understand German culture and history, this is the book for you (it's also fun to read).

- *Old World – New World, Craig Storti*
  This well written and very useful book informs the reader about the differences between Americans and the British, the French and the Germans. It is explained very well and easily readable. The book uses example multicultural dialogues and analyses them to show the consequences of cultural differences. These differences are explained with good historical background and reasons. The explanation of the development of the American culture as compared to the European culture is a valuable attribute of this book. The dialogues are mainly from the business environment, but the analysis presents good overall cultural information. However, the section about the French is a bit short and repetitive. The book is mainly aimed at people of the above-mentioned nationalities, but I'm sure it can be just as helpful if you come from another country and want to learn about any of those four nations.

- *Doing Business with Germans: Their Perception, Our Perception, Sylvia Schroll-Machl*
  This is a very thorough and methodical book that gives a detailed view of German values and how they influence business, together with several examples. The writing style is – in my opinion – too academic, but so far this is the most useful book on business with Germans and there surely is a wealth of information included.

2. Internet

Fortunately the internet has vastly increased ways of obtaining information. Helpful expat websites are blooming, some of them of a more general nature, some of them dealing with special countries. There are also some links relating to special subjects in the relevant chapters of this book.

a. Expat Links

• www.expatexchange.com – forum, country-specific information and articles as well as links covering many areas (cars, banks, organizations, insurance, housing etc.)

• www.expatforum.com – a big and active forum for general expat issues, with several subforums for different countries

• www.expatsblog.com – a collection of expat blogs from all over the world, sorted by country and city. At the time of writing this, there are more than 100 expat blogs on living in Germany

• http://europa.eu – information for citizens of the European Union on living, working etc. in other EU countries

• www.britishexpats.com – as the name already implies, this site is aimed at British expats. It has a forum and several blogs

• www.internations.org – a big online community of expats. You get information about the city where you live and the activities Internations organizes there, there are forums and you can find and contact other expats

b. Germany-related links

• www.virtualtourist.com/Europe/Germany – Tourist info, very detailed and informative, with tips from travelers, also includes culture/behavioral tips and city guides

• www.tatsachen-ueber-deutschland.de – the information handbook of the German Embassy

- www.make-it-in-germany.com – a comprehensive information website by the German government

- www.expatica.com/de – The "Germany" site of expatica.com. News, links and information

- www.howtogermany.com – Links and information about different aspects of living in Germany

- www.german-way.com – Links and information for expats to Germany, Austria and Switzerland

- www.toytowngermany.com – English-speaking online community of expats in Germany

c. Regional links

Some of the general forums and websites mentioned above also have regional information, subforums or sub-groups.

Berlin
- www.berlinfo.com – An international guide for Berlin, covering all aspects such as administrative matters, health, culture, arts, family, food etc.

- www.berlin.de – official website of Berlin with plenty of information on living in and traveling to Berlin

Düsseldorf, Nordrhein-Westfalen
- www.newcomers-network.de – information on the area, a forum, events and more

- www.duesseldorf.de – official website of Düsseldorf with plenty of information on living in and traveling to Düsseldorf

Frankfurt am Main, Hessen
- www.frankfurt.de – the official website of Frankfurt with plenty of information on living in and travelling to Frankfurt

- www.newcomers-network.de – information on the area, a forum, events and more

Hamburg
- http://english.hamburg.de – Tourist information (including musicals, special hotel deals etc.) as well as a useful section called "Newcomers Service" with information about living in Hamburg, administrative procedures and services for citizens.

Munich, Bavaria
- www.bayern.de – General information about Bavaria as well as further links, covering political, administrative as well as tourist information (click on "Other languages" in the top menu to get to your language)

- www.muenchen.de – the official website of Munich with plenty of information on living in and travelling to Munich

- www.muenchen.de/int/en/tourism/important-information/services-english.html – direct link to English-speaking services in Munich

- www.newcomers-network.de – information on the area, a forum, events and more

Stuttgart, Baden-Württemberg
- www.stuttgart-tourist.de – General information about Stuttgart, covering hotels, events, shopping, food and transportation

- www.stuttgart.de – the official website of Stuttgart with plenty of information on living in and travelling to Stuttgart

3. Clubs

Most of the larger cities in Germany have a substantial expat population and therefore you will find all kinds of international clubs in most of them. These clubs not only are a great help with getting to know other expats and mastering daily life in a foreign country, they are also valuable sources of information prior to a move. Usually, they have websites with contact information and links, so don't hesitate to mail or phone them if you have any questions. All of the expats that mentioned having joined an international club in the questionnaires said that these clubs were a tremendous help and life-savers.

Many of them have sub groups for people with special interests, they publish newsletters with information about events in the club and in the area and they also offer interesting possibilities for volunteer work and business contacts.

You can find them by doing an internet search on "expat club" or "international clubs" in your area. If a club is labled "British Club" or "American Club", it does not mean that they don't accept members of other nationalities.

4. Companies (in case of an international assignment)

If you or your spouse come to Germany on an international assignment, usually the company sending you abroad will take care of immigration matters and also provide you with some general information. However, every company transferee and/or accompanying spouse who filled out and returned the questionnaire pointed out that although administrative matters and all issues concerning the move were generally handled well by the company, they were not provided with any information at all/with sufficient information about daily life matters. From my own experience in expatriate management, I know very well that this is true and that often neither the companies in the home countries nor the companies in the host countries supply their assignees with such information. They rely on the relocation agencies to deal with this, or they simply don't have the time to compile information lists or packages. It also greatly depends on whether your company has a special department dealing with international assignments or not. Employees in such a department have more time and experience to put together an information package or at least a link list. Do not hesitate to ask for such a list in the company you work in / your spouse works in, and if such a list is unknown to the company, you might suggest, as an incentive, that such a list / package should be initiated. Consequently, you could share useful links with the company.

If a company sends you or your spouse to another country, it will almost always reimburse you for any moving and visa costs. Most companies have limits for moving expenses, depending on company policy and also on the length of your assignment. They might also ask you to move with a certain moving company or to get some cost estimates from several companies first.

The amount of assistance you get depends on the size of the company and as mentioned before also often on whether they have a special international assignments department or not. Most companies have an assignment policy, so you should ask for that policy to find out what benefits you are entitled to and which costs you will have to bear yourself. This prevents confusion and unpleasant financial surprises. You should also find out how far the company supports you with tax issues and health insurance, as those issues are usually tricky when you go abroad. Help with the house hunting or with the provision for temporary housing is also extremely valuable.

It can also be helpful to ask your company to get you in touch with other assignees that already are (or have been) in Germany. Usually, that is no problem as expats within a company are supportive and willing to exchange information with their colleagues. If you are an accompanying spouse you might feel left out in the preparations as many companies tend to concentrate on the needs of the assignee. I always told our assignees that their spouses were welcome to call me if they had any questions, and many of them did. In a previous company where I worked I also tried to encourage the spouses to exchange email addresses with other spouses living in the same country and generally they appreciated this method of getting into touch with other spouses in the same situation. I know of companies where expat spouses organized their own network among themselves, so this is also an option.

5. Relocation Agencies

Many companies make use of relocation agencies, especially for bureaucratic matters. Although private persons can also engage relocation agencies, some might shy away from the costs. Relocation agencies offer all kinds of services, the core services are assisting with visas, work and residence permits as well as the registration of utilities or phone. Supplementary services are house hunting and usually there is also the chance for a small tour of your new home city, information packages and in some cases, they also assist with the search for craftsmen, domestic servants and in shopping matters.

When you come to Germany in the course of an international assignment through your company, the services a relocation agency offers you are determined by your employer and usually only cover the core services mentioned above. Relocation agencies can be extremely helpful and many make an effort to provide the best possible service. If that is not the case, do not hesitate to inform your employer. Your employer is interested in finding out whether his relocation money is well spent and he therefore welcomes any adequate feedback. One respondent to the questionnaire informed me that the relocation agency hired for them by her husband's employer was supposed to help them with the purchase of a car. Unfortunately, the relocation agent merely directed them to a street where there were several car dealers located, but did not help with the purchase or the registration process.

If you are unsure what services are covered (and to what extent; for example whether the relocation agency is actually supposed to accompany you to a car dealer or if it should merely supply you with addresses), ask your employer.

6. Universities and Academic Exchange Agencies

Students who go to study abroad independent of international exchange programs will usually only get help from the university in the host country. Most German universities now have websites that are partly in English or special website sections for international students. Some of them also offer good and useful guides about life in Germany or at that university. In many other cases, the information will simply include facts about health insurance and housing on and off campus. Students who have filled out the questionnaire affirm the answers made by expats on an intercompany transfer – they often missed information about daily life situations and bureaucracy matters. Generally, students have to find their own accommodation, which can be difficult coming from another country and not speaking German. In such cases, you should try to get accommodation on campus in student housing (*Studentenwohnheim*), as it will save you the hassle with lease/tenancy contract negotiations and other matters in connection with the search for accommodation on the free market.

Check out these websites for further information:
• www.daad.de – the website of the German Academic Exchange Service

• www.hochschulkompass.de – here you can find information on German institutions of higher education in English

• www.internationale-studierende.de – plenty of useful information for students coming to Germany

7. House Hunting

House hunting can be a difficult task, largely depending on which area you want to live in. I was surprised that about half of the respondents to the questionnaires stated that they didn't think finding appropriate accommodation difficult. Generally, those who had little trouble finding somewhere suitable to live had been supported by their company, who had appointed a relocation agency to look for houses and/or cover real estate brokers fees, which greatly facilitates finding proper accommodation. Real estate agents usually find you a house relatively quickly, but they are extremely expensive and therefore not the first choice for the majority of expats.

The housing situation is extremely difficult in most big cities cities – they usually have the largest expat communities – and their surroundings. Rents are accordingly high and finding the right place to live can be a tiring experience.

So, how can you find a place to live in Germany?

a. Buying or Renting

First, you should decide whether you want to buy or rent a property. Generally, you will find that renting is the better option, as buying a house in Germany is usually more complicated and expensive than, for example, in the United

States or in the United Kingdom. This is why you will notice that renting is far more common in Germany. Particularly if you are only planning to live in Germany for a few years, renting is most likely to be the better solution from a financial viewpoint, as profits from house sales are not high and taxes have to be paid if a house is sold within 10 years after purchase.

b. Buying

If you do decide to buy a house, the two main information sources are real estate agents and newspapers. If you use the services of a real estate agent, be aware that they demand commission fees which differ regionally, but are usually between 2 – 4 % of the sale price. The real estate agent can only demand a commission if he himself concludes the sales contract! If he merely shows you the property, but another real estate agent or a third person concludes the sales contract, the first estate agent is not entitled to a commission. It is advisable to engage the help of a native speaker when negotiating with a real estate agent. Real estate agents also place ads in newspapers, so if a house or apartment is put up for sale by a private person it will usually contain the phrase von privat. In this case, there is no need to pay a commission, as you deal with the seller directly.

If you find a property you like and agree on the sale with the vendor, there are certain formal requirements you have to adhere to in order to guarantee the validity of the contract. The contract has to be certified by a notary public. This encompasses the contract being signed in the presence of the notary public after he has informed the parties involved of the legal implications of the contract. If you are not familiar with the German language you should hire an interpreter to ensure that you have really understood the terms of the contract.

After the sale is final, an entry in the land register/real-estate register (*Grundbuch*) is made, stating you as the new owner. It is the entry in the Grundbuch that establishes your ownership! The register also indicates if there are any third-party rights to the property, e.g. a lease (a lease is binding to subsequent owners!). If a third-party right is not entered in the register and it is unknown to you at the time of purchase, that right cannot be asserted against you.

c. Renting

You can also search for property to rent through real estate agents and internet or newspaper ads. Depending on the situation on the housing market, landlords choose tenants just a few hours after ads appear. The best method to find a place to live is by word of mouth, maybe through colleagues (especially expat colleagues who leave Germany might be happy to find a successor for their rented property).

The most common way of looking for accommodation is the internet. Robert Lederman, an expat from Canada, comments that he had no problem finding a cheap apartment in Frankfurt via www.immobilienscout24.de, the largest real estate website in Germany.

The ads with their many abbreviations are sometimes even difficult for Germans to understand, so this applies even more so to someone who is not familiar with the German language. Therefore, please find below a short overview of the most important terms and abbreviations in real estate ads. If you are from the United States or United Kingdom, you are probably used to apartments being described as "one bedroom" or "two bedroom" apartments. In Germany, apartments are described by the total of rooms (the kitchen and bathrooms not counting as rooms), so a two-bedroom-apartment could be a "three-room-apartment" (*Dreizimmerwohnung*).

Abbre-viation	German Term	English Term / Remarks
2-Zi-Whg	2-Zimmer-Wohnung	2-room-apartment
AB	Altbau	Old building (usually pre-WWII)
App.	Appartement	Apartment
Balk.	Balkon	Balcony
DG	Dachgeschoss	Loft, top floor
DHH	Doppelhaushälfte	Semi-detached house
Du.	Dusche	Shower
EFH	Einfamilienhaus	Detached house

Abbre-viation	German Term	English Term / Remarks
EG	Erdgeschoss	Ground floor (=1st floor in the US, in Germany, the first floor would be equivalent to an American 2nd floor)
Einb.-Kü.	Einbauküche	Fitted kitchen
Gara.	Garage	Garage
Gashzg.	Gasheizung	Gas heating
Hs.	Haus	House
Hzg.	Heizung	Heating
Immob.	Immobilienmakler	Ad placed by a real estate agent
inkl.	Inklusive	Inclusive
Kaut./K/Kt	Kaution	Security deposit
KDB	Küche, Diele, Bad	Kitchen, hall, bathroom
KM	Kaltmiete	Rent without utilities
Kochn. / KN	Kochnische	Kitchenette
Kü.	Küche	Kitchen
mbl.	Möbliert	Furnished
Mte.	Miete	Rent
NB	Neubau	New house
NK	Nebenkosten	Utilities
NR	Nichtraucher	Non-smoker
öZH	Ölzentralheizung	Oil central heating
OG	Obergeschoss	Upper floor
Part.	Parterre	Ground floor (see EG)
qm	Quadratmeter	Square metres
RH	Reihenhaus	Terraced / row house
ruh. Lage	ruhige Lage	Quiet area (sometimes it just says "ruh." meaning quiet)
Stadtr.	Stadtrand	Outskirts of the town / city
Terr.	Terasse	Terrace
WM	Warmmiete	Rent including most / all utilities

Abbre-viation	German Term	English Term / Remarks
Wohnfl.	Wohnfläche	Living space (usually used in connection with qm)
Zi.	Zimmer	Room
Zentr.	Zentrum	City Centre / Downtown
ZH	Zentralheizung	Central Heating
ZKB	Zimmer, Küche, Bad	Room(s), kitchen, bathroom (3ZKB would mean three rooms, plus kitchen and bathroom)
zzgl. NK	Zuzüglich Nebenkosten	Plus utilities

Make sure to inform yourself about the different areas of your new home town. A cheap apartment is far less desirable if you end up in an unpleasant area or far away from the city center without sufficient means of public transport. As Maureen Chase, an expat from the USA, puts it: "Ask Germans where the agreeable places are to live, places that are convenient to your lifestyle and needs. Ask other expats, too."

If you are transferring with a company, ask people in the German company location whether they can recommend areas, or if you take on the services of a relocation agency, ask them about different residential areas. Contacting international clubs in that area, expat forums or generally the internet are also good options for finding out about the best areas to live in.

You will find that furnished apartments are scarce, this also applies to student housing. Furniture rental is practically unknown in Germany, so be prepared to have to completely furnish your new home. Most German houses or apartments don't have a built-in kitchen, so don't be surprised if your new kitchen is just an empty room. You will then have to buy a kitchen and when you move out again maybe the next tenant will be happy to buy it from you. Sometimes a kitchen is included or can be bought from the previous tenant (you might occasionally discover that buying certain fitted items or furniture is conditional for the rent contract). If you intend to buy something from the previous tenant (in case of fitted kitchens, it could be recommendable!) make sure prices are adequate.

Built-in closets are unknown in Germany, Germans buy cupboards instead. Many furniture stores offer complete bedroom furniture comprising a bed and a cupboard/several matching cupboards. You also have a choice of special furniture for corridors and hallways, very functional for storing outdoor clothing and shoes.

d. Rent Contract (Mietvertrag) and Rent Law (Mietrecht)

Once you find a property you like, you phone the landlord to make an appointment for viewing it. It is possible that the landlord makes one appointment for everyone interested in the property (especially in larger cities where the market is tight and apartments scarce).

If you want to rent the property and it is still available, the landlord may ask you for a reference of income, or even a letter from your employer stating that you are able to pay the rent. It might be useful to have such documents with you when you view the property.

Be aware that lease contracts are usually long and quite complicated, so it is advisable to take someone along who is fluent in German to ensure that you understand the contract. Also clarify what extra charges/ancillary rental costs will be added to the rent, e.g. for water and utilities you have to take care of yourself.

There are several other points to consider:

*   Security deposit (*Kaution*): the security deposit - which usually amounts to two or three months' rent (rent law forbids security deposits that are higher than three month's rent!) - is there to ensure that you leave the property in good order at the end of your lease. As one of the questionnaire respondents advises: "Inspect and agree on the condition of the apartment before moving in, photograph or get the owner to sign a paper agreeing existing damage. The negotiations to get your deposit back can be difficult otherwise." (also see below: *Übergabe*)

- Generally, the lease contract requires you to renovate the property before you leave it and the security deposit is only paid back if that is done properly. The landlord has to return the deposit with interest. Nowadays, it is more common to move into an apartment that is in a non-renovated condition, so that the new tenant is free to paint and decorate according to his own taste, or to conduct any necessary renovation work himself. This means that he does not have to renovate the property before moving out. In such cases, the security deposit is paid back unless there are damages to the property. Robert Lederman highly recommends this option as he had to spend a lot of money on painting his Stuttgart apartment before moving out: "We agreed to paint at the end rather than when we moved in. I spoke with several people and they all said to let the landlord do it. It was very unlikely that we could get it up to his standards. (...) If you are paying for the move out of pocket, avoid using estate agents and if possible agree to leave the flat unpainted. Will save you a lot of money."

- Sometimes a landlord will ask you to put the deposit in a savings account (*Sparkonto*) and then hand the savings book (*Sparbuch*) of the *Sparkonto* over to him. If you leave the apartment in an acceptable condition, the landlord will return the *Sparbuch* to you.

- House rules (*Hausordnung*): apartment buildings generally have house rules which are indicated in the lease contract and to which you must adhere. Even if there are no house rules, there are some general rules everybody should follow. The most important one is the Ruhezeit, meaning that everybody is to avoid creating noise disturbances between 1 – 3 pm (in some areas) and 10 pm – 7 am on week-days (12 am - 7 am on Saturdays) and all day on Sundays and holidays (also see page 34). If you live in an apartment building, barbecuing on your balcony is usually strictly forbidden.

- Notice period / term of lease: some leases are for a specified period of 3 or 5 years and it is very hard to end such a contract at an earlier date, as the statutory notice period is usually suspended for the duration of such contracts. However, the notice period exclusion must be specifically stated in the lease contract! If this is not the case, the statutory notice period applies. If you need to get out of such a contract and you want to avoid severe fines or continuous rent payments after moving out, it is advisable to have your contract examined by a lawyer specialized in rent law or by someone in a *Mieterverein* (association of tenants, they usually ask you to become a member for a small fee, but it's worth it), to check whether you can use the notice period or not. Some contracts allow you to get out prematurely if you find a successor for the flat (the landlord has to approve of the person!). Even if the lease does not specify a certain period of tenancy, the statuary notice period in Germany is quite long - generally three months. The notice period for the landlord might even be longer, as it extends with the length of the lease contract. The statutory notice period for landlords is three months for lease contracts up to five years, then it is extended to six months up to a term of tenancy of eight years, after which it is extended to nine months. The notice period for tenants is three months without exception, independent of the length of the lease.

- *Übergabe*: When you take over the property from the previous tenant and when you leave the apartment, an *Übergabe* (=transfer) takes place, which means that the landlord inspects the apartment in your presence and together with the previous / next tenant in order to check the state of the premises.

Issues that are not mentioned in the contract are regulated by the German rent law, which you can find in the BGB (*Bürgerliches Gesetzbuch*, the main civil legal code of Germany). Generally, the German rent law is very tenant-friendly and a recent revision strengthened tenants' rights even more.

e. Utilities

Once you have found a nice place to live and you have settled all contract matters, you should take care of having all your utilities connected. First, you need to find out which utilities you have to take care of yourself and which ones are taken care of by your landlord (in apartment buildings, the water supply and the garbage collection is usually organized by the landlord). Some companies provide several utilities. Nowadays, people have a much wider variety of companies to choose from for connecting/installing their utilities, especially with regard to electricity and phones; here again, colleagues and neighbors might be able to advise you as to the best choice.

Ensure that all outstanding bills are paid by the previous tenants so that you will not be made responsible for their debts. During the *Übergabe*, make a point of reading all the utility meters and make a note of them!

Water, electricity and gas are supplied by local providers, the names and phone numbers of which can be supplied by your landlord, the previous tenant, or neighbors and colleagues.

In order to get your electricity, gas and water connected, you generally need to fill out a form with certain details (address, date of moving in etc.) as well as the moving out date and name of the previous tenant. (You can ask the providing company to send you a form or tell you where to find a customer center. Most companies provide the possibility of downloading the form in the internet or of even carrying out the whole application process by internet.) You also have to provide them with the meter reading on the day you move in (some companies might prefer to send someone to do the meter reading, but generally it is sufficient to inform them of the reading. If you fail to do this, the company might send someone and charge you for that). After the company receives the form, they will send you a confirmation and inform you of the monthly anticipation payments (sometimes the payments only have to be made every two months) you have to make. This sum is adjusted annually (according to the amount used in the previous year) after the meters have been read by an employee of the company. You will be informed of the dates for the yearly meter reading, so you should either be at home or ensure that someone can let the person in, as they may charge you if a second visit is made necessary.

You can either transfer payments each month/second month to the company's account or you can give them permission for a direct debit (see article about financial matters for an explanation of payment methods).

III. First Impressions & General Information

1. First Impressions

First impressions can either positively or negatively influence the whole stay abroad, but they are usually revised or at least altered once the host country is known better. When I went to Philadelphia for my studies, my first impression was very negative. During the ride from the airport to the hotel I didn't get to see the best part of the city and as the hotel wasn't in a good area either, my first impression of Philadelphia was that of a shabby run-down city and I was close to regretting my decision. I later found out that this first picture was shared by many others who didn't know Philadelphia very well. However, after a while my fellow students (all of them coming from other countries) and I made the same experience — we got to know the city better and in the end we all loved it as we had had a chance to take a glimpse behind the initial "picture" and to explore the beauties Philadelphia had to offer. So, if your first impression of Germany is negative — don't give up right away, chances are you will find many things you like. About one third of the questionnaire respondents had a negative first impression, one third a positive impression and for one third it was fairly neutral. Most of those that didn't have a positive first impression later found many things they described as positive and also often revised negative first impressions.

A point that came up frequently was that Germans seemed unfriendly, inflexible and bureaucratic. Compared to many other nations Germans are in fact more reserved and foreigners (even Germans, by the way!) often complain about the lack of customer service, although there has definitely been an improvement regarding this. There are many laws and regulations and as Sarah Happel, an accompanying spouse from the US, pointed out, people who don't know you might nevertheless draw your attention to you breaking any laws and/or regulations, even if you have done so inadvertently. She said that one of the German sentences she heard most often during her first months in Germany was *"Das geht nicht!"* ("You can't do that!")

So, it is easy to gain a negative first impression of Germany and Germans if you are confronted with an unfriendly sales person, an exaggeratingly correct neighbor or glum-faced people on the street just after your arrival in the country. Just don't let this discourage you or convince you that this is all you will ever encounter in Germany. As many expats later discovered, Germans can be just as friendly and fun as any other people in spite of their initially reserved manner, it just takes longer to find that out. There will be more about German peculiarities on pages 74 - 96 and you will see that first impressions can be reversed.

Bureaucracy is widespread in Germany and will be dealt with more intensively in a separate chapter starting on page 97. As a foreigner coming to live in Germany, you will experience bureaucracy here as more complicated and stressful than most Germans do, simply because you need to apply for documents such as work and residence permits, which doesn't affect Germans generally. People who have never lived in a foreign country cannot imagine the many details that have to be considered in the course of an international move. So this experience can come as quite a shock, especially if (as in most cases) newcomers are not familiar with the German language at that point, which makes handling administrative matters even more complicated. Alice Waldron, who came to Germany from the United Kingdom for her studies, mentioned how shocked she was by being confronted with so many unknown bureaucratic matters. This was the first impression she had of Germany and she said: "Getting registered and 'settled' was more complicated and stressful than I imagined."

Fortunately, once you are finished with the initial registrations, permits etc., the worst part of your bureaucratic involvement with German authorities is usually over. If you are lucky to have a relocation agency to take care of many details, this is of course immensely helpful and can make the transition more amicable, which is why most companies at least take over the expenses for the initial registration and application for work and residence permits through a relocation agent.

A smooth transition definitely helps towards winning a favourable first impression of your new home country. If you don't have to worry about administrative matters, house hunting or finding the right shops and doctors, you have more time to discover the positive things and to enjoy the experience of beginning a new and exciting phase in life. Maureen Chase, an accompanying spouse from the US, fortunately had the chance to enjoy her new surroundings quickly. When asked about her first impression of Germany, she said: "Great, because it was a new place. It didn't seem hard to find the grocery store to get our essentials so that was good. And, there were things to do on the weekend (...) with our son. Everything seemed so compact and easy here compared to the more spread out U.S. cities."

Some expats also noted that larger cities, especially Frankfurt, are somewhat "americanized" already, combining the new with the familiar.

As banal as it may seem, the time of year you arrive in Germany can have a large impact on your first impression. Expats who arrived in the winter often stated that their first impression of their new location was dreary and depressing due to the cold gloomy weather. This is entirely understandable as hardly any place is enticing during that kind of weather, but it should be kept in mind that the weather has this strong impact. Expats who arrived in Germany in the summer immediately noted the many cafés and beer gardens and of course the beer, or as an expat from Australia put it: "The Germans drive really fast and drink a lot of beer". It was interesting to discover how German beer and chocolate seemed to help improve the first impression, so that many expats were quite eager to try out German food specialities.

As you can see, first impressions can vary a lot and are influenced by small matters such as the weather, help with settling in and of course being informed about what to expect. You can't "steer" your first impression, but if it turns out negative or less positive than you expected, remember it is only just that – a first impression.

2. The Basics about Germany

A good knowledge of the country you are going to move to is crucial in avoiding a culture shock. So, what do you know about Germany? What do you need to know and what do you want to know? A large part of this book will concentrate on the German culture, how it is perceived by expats and what is behind it. You will read about German behavior and customs and hopefully grasp a better understanding of it. Another large section is dedicated to daily life issues that will confront you – opening a bank account, doing food shopping or even getting stamps. But first, I want to give you some general information about this country that will be your home, kind of a first introduction. It is just an overview and if you care to know more about a certain subject, there are many books about German politics or history that will give you a more detailed background.

Now, let's assume you know absolutely nothing about Germany yet. What would be the absolute basic facts about this country? Here they are:

Germany covers an area of 357,021 sq km (greatest distance north-south: 880 km, greatest distance east-west 750 km) and with 82 million people (10% of which are not Germans) has the second-largest population in Europe. About 30% of the population are Protestants, 30% are Catholics, about 5% (estimate) Muslims and about 35% are either unaffiliated or belong to other religions.

Germany borders nine (!) countries, which are: Austria, Belgium, Czech Republic, Denmark, France, Luxembourg, the Netherlands, Poland and Switzerland.

The head of the German government is the Chancellor (*Bundeskanzlerin*) Angela Merkel (since 2005), the Head of State is the President (*Bundespräsident*) Joachim Gauck (since 2012). When you are reading this, the new Bundespräsident will have been elected and it will probably be Frank-Walter Steinmeier.

The capital of Germany is Berlin, even though the former capital, Bonn, still retains many administrative functions and several ministries.

Germany consists of 16 states (*Bundesländer*): Baden-Württemberg, Bayern, Berlin, Brandenburg, Bremen, Hamburg, Hessen, Mecklenburg-Vorpommern, Niedersachsen, Nordrhein-Westfalen, Rheinland-Pfalz, Saarland, Sachsen, Sachsen-Anhalt, Schleswig-Holstein and Thüringen.

The national language is German, however in many of the German Bundesländer people have diverse and distinctive dialects, which are sometimes hard to understand even for Germans from other Bundesländer.

The largest cities (and those that usually have a larger expat population) are (from north to south): Hamburg, Berlin, Düsseldorf, Köln (Cologne), Frankfurt, Wiesbaden, Stuttgart and München (Munich).

The most important national holiday is October 3, which commemorates the reunification of East and West Germany on October 3, 1990. Since the reunification the German Constitution (Grundgesetz), which has been applied to West Germany since its ratification in 1949, is valid for the united Germany.

On page 90 you will learn how the whole of Germany basically "stands still" during its national holidays. Apart from October 3, other German national holidays are:

- Neujahr (New Year's Day), January 1
- *Ostern* (Easter) – comprising of *Karfreitag* (Good Friday), *Ostersonntag* (Easter Sunday) and *Ostermontag* (Easter Monday), yes, all of them are holidays!
- *Maifeiertag*, May 1 – the Maifeiertag is mainly a political holiday, with many demonstrations organised by unions and workers' organisations. More pleasant traditions (mainly adhered to in rural areas) are the "Tanz in den Mai" (parties and dances taking place on April 30, to 'dance into the May') and the Maibäume (May trees), small trees, usually decorated with ribbons that are put up in the marketplace. In some villages young men climb onto the roof of the house in which their girlfriends live and place a May tree on it as a sign of their affection. I remember driving through rural areas as a child and my mother and I would count the many Maibäume we saw during the ride.
- *Christi Himmelfahrt* (Ascension of Christ) – taking place on the 40th day after Easter, always on a Thursday, which encourages many employees to take the Friday off as well to enjoy a long weekend.
- *Pfingsten* (Pentecost) – taking place on the 50th day after Easter and comprising of *Pfingstsonntag* (Pentecost Sunday) and *Pfingstmontag* (Pentecost Monday)
- *Weihnachten* (Christmas) – National holidays are

December 25 and December 26, even though many companies give their employees an extra day off on December 24. In Germany, presents are exchanged on Christmas Eve (*Heiligabend*), whereas December 25 is often dedicated to family visits. Read more about Christmas traditions and Christmas markets on pages 93 - 95.

There are also holidays that only occur in certain Bundesländer, usually the Catholic ones. If you work in Bavaria, you can enjoy more holidays than in Hessen or Hamburg (if you live and work in different *Bundesländer*, you should be aware that you are only entitled to the holidays valid in the *Bundesland* you work in, not to the holidays in the *Bundesland* you live in). These regional holidays are January 6 (Epiphany / *Dreikönigstag*), the second Thursday after Pfingsten (Corpus Christi / *Fronleichnam*), August 15 (Assumption of the Virgin Mary / *Mariä Himmelfahrt*), October 31 (Reformation Day / *Reformationstag*), November 1 (All Saints' Day / *Allerheiligen*) and the Day of Prayer and Repentance / *Buß- und Bettag* in November, which used to be a national holiday, but fell prey to the financing of the nursing insurance and is now only a holiday in Sachsen (Saxonia).

As English is mandatory in school, many Germans, especially the post-war generation, speak it quite fluently, especially in the large cities in Western Germany.

Germany has a diverse countryside, ranging from the flatlands of the North to the Alps in the South; forests and woodland cover 31% of the country.

The climate is temperate, generally with warm summers and cold winters (summer high: 25°C/77°F, winter low: -5°C/23°F). Rain falls throughout the year, usually there is snow in winter but not for prolonged periods.

3. A Short Overview of German History

As you will read about German culture later on, many facets of German behavior and culture arise from its history. Two obvious and related consequences of Germany's past are the lack of a real national identity and a hesitant approach to patriotism. I once walked through Munich with an American friend and he told me how surprised he was that there were no German flags to be seen anywhere. As he came from a country where the Stars and Stripes are omnipresent, it seemed highly unusual to him for a country not to display the national flag. You will definitely not see an abundance of German flags. They are generally limited to government buildings and can sometimes be seen at the entrances of large international companies. The only occasion when people really show the black-red-gold stripes of the German flag is during the football season. When the World Championship took place in Germany in 2006, the flag was displayed more widely than ever before after the last war (see also page 58). - The national anthem is also sung far less often than in the US or in several other countries. Whereas patriotism was looked upon in a favorable way after Germany became a united country in 1871, the events between 1933 and 1945 (when patriotism and an abundant display of flags were basically ordered by law) have made Germans shy away from it.

Whereas you are probably quite familiar with German history after 1933, there is of course far more to it, as this country has a history that goes back much farther. Following is a short summary of the development of Germany. Each section ends with an overview of sights in Germany that refer to the respective time period, so that if you are interested in a certain period, you will know where to travel to in order to learn more about it. Of course, this overview is not complete, but it gives you a good first impression.

a. The Beginning (pre-historical times – 482)

The first Germans (of course they were not really Germans in the historical sense, but rather the first human beings whose remains were discovered on German soil) were called "*Homo Heidelbergensis*". As you can tell from the name, their remains were found close to Heidelberg. They lived in that region around 600,000 years ago. About 100,000 years ago, they were followed by the *Neandertaler*, the remains of which were exposed in the Neandertal close to Düsseldorf. The first inhabitants whose lives are actually documented in history are the *Germanen* (Teutons) and the *Kelten* (Celts). The *Germanen* lived in the northern part of Germany as we know it today and the *Kelten* inhabited the area of what is today South Germany. The German *Kelten* gave the Roman invaders a hard time, but they were eventually conquered around 50 B.C. They assimilated well to Roman culture, whereas the Germanen were not inclined to do so at all. They withstood all Roman attempts to conquer them and never adopted the Roman way of life. The most prominent example of Germanic resistance against the Roman conquerors is the Varus Battle (*Varusschlacht*), in which **Hermann (Arminian) the Cherusker** (the Cherusker being a tribe of the *Germanen*) led his people towards an amazing victory against the Roman troops under Publius Quinctilius Varus. This battle has become a legend throughout history and is often seen as a symbol for the fight against tyranny. It is also called "*Schlacht im Teutoburger Wald*" (Battle in the Teutoburger Forest) as it was long believed that this was the location of the battle. There is no proof that the battle took place in the region that is today called Teutoburger Wald, in fact scientists have several theories about the location. The by now most popular theory – and in my opinion the one that makes most sense – is that the battle took place in Kalkriese, near Osnabrück, where several artifacts supporting the theory have been found.

For a long time, the rivers Rhine and Donau formed the eastern and northern borders of Roman expansion. These borders moved slightly farther to the north and east in 83 AD when the construction of the **Limes** was started soon afterwards along these borderlines. The Limes consisted of watchtowers connected by a fence, later it was strengthened more and more, until it had turned into a large and strong wall around 213 AD. It was, however, not an inpermeable border; trade and friendly exchanges were the norm.

The regions south and west of the Limes belonged to the Romans and numerous cities that still exist today were founded or developed by the Romans. Many were originally military bases where soldiers settled with their families. Typical examples of such cities are Augsburg (*Augusta Vindelicorum*), Köln (*Colonia Claudia Ara Agrippinensium*), Mainz (*Mogontiacum*), Trier (*Augusta Treverorum*) or Xanten (*Castra Vetera*).

From 250 – 450 AD the *Völkerwanderung* – the migration of

different tribes – uprooted Germany. A chief example of such a migration illustrates the action of the Huns, who chased the *Goten* (Goths) from western Asia to Europe, as far west as today's Spain. A time of unrest began, ending Roman rule over South-West Germany. The way was free for a new Empire – the *Frankenreich* (Franconian Empire).

If you care to learn more about the life of the early German tribes or want to visit some of the many Roman remains, here are a few suggestions:

- Visit the excellent museum for *Pfahlbauten* in Unteruhldingen at Lake Constance and see how people lived thousands of years ago – www.pfahlbauten.de (also in English)
- *Hermannsdenkmal*, a statue showing Hermann the Cherusker, which can be found at the Grotenburg close to Detmold – www.hermannsdenkmal.de (only in German)
- The *Limesstraße* (Limes street) leading you to the main attractions along the Limes (for more information see page 134)
- A Roman open-air museum can be found in Hechingen-Stein (between Stuttgart and Lake Constance). It features an excavated and restored Roman villa – www.villa-rustica.de (also in English)
- Roman remains can be seen in Augsburg (www.augsburg.de – also in English), Mainz (www.mainz.de – also in English), Speyer (www.speyer.de – also in English), Köln (www.koeln.de - also in English), Xanten (www.xanten.de – only in German) and especially Trier (www.trier.de – also in English)

b. From the Franconian Empire to the first German Empire (482 – 919)

The Franconian Empire extended across today's France, Belgium and the Netherlands as well as a large part of today's Germany. The Franconians, who were very Catholic and also demanded this dedication to Catholicism of their subjects, started to spread over Europe in the 250s. The three most famous heads of this empire were grandfather, father and son: Karl Martell (714 – 741), Pippin der Jüngere (741 - 768) and

Karl der Große (768 – 814). They played a large part in strengthening and enlarging the empire. Karl der Große (Karl the Great) was the most influential of the three. He was an impressive tall and sportive man who resided in Aachen. He made a strong reputation for himself internationally – although his reputation was extremely negative in Sachsen (Saxonia), which had to suffer under his brutal and enduring attacks. Karl der Große propagated the Catholic faith in a cruel manner, often leaving his victims to decide solely between reverting to Catholicism or being killed. Nevertheless, at the time of his death, he was highly regarded due to his many successes as well as for his efforts to improve business and education throughout the empire. His reign is also considered the beginning of the *Römische Reich Deutscher Nation* (the German Roman Empire), which would last until 1806.

Through wars, Karl der Große managed to extend his Empire even further, so that at the time of his death it covered the largest part of Western Europe. Before his death, he had divided his empire into three parts, as he realized that its pure vastness made it almost impossible for one person to rule over it successfully. After the division, today's Germany then belonged to the East Franconian Empire for several years.

After about a hundred years of rivalries, wars and further divisions of the Empire, **Heinrich I.** was crowned King of Germany in 919. This is considered to be the beginning of the German Empire, as the East Franconian Empire was renamed **Empire of the Germans** (*Regnum teutonicorum*) during the reign of Heinrich I.

Noteworthy buildings of the Franconian Empire are:
- The Pfalz in Aachen (part of the Cathedral), where one can see the throne of Karl der Große as well as the famous Karlsschrein. (www.aachendom.de – only in German)
- Torhalle Kloster Lorsch (www.kloster-lorsch.de – also in English)
- Convent of Corvey (www.schloss-corvey.de – also in English)
- Kloster Brunshausen in Bad Gandersheim (www.bad-gandersheim-online.de – only in German)

c.   The Crusades and the High Middle Ages (919 - 1273)

After Heinrich I. died in 936, his son Otto became king and founded a dynasty of German kings called Otto – the **Ottonen**, who led Germany into the High Middle Ages. The High Middle Ages were the time of large impressive cathedrals and convents, going hand in hand with a deep piety of the people. This deep piety also had unpleasant consequences like the crusades, the first of which took place from 1096 – 1099, the seventh (and last one) was in 1270. For almost two hundred years, German kings and knights went to Israel (as we know it today) to "free" the Holy Land from Muslims. During that time, a whole German colonialist culture sprouted up in Israel, complete with crusaders' castles, Christian religion and knights. The battles against those of a different belief was not limited to the Holy Land. On their way the crusaders, soon joined by local mobs, started vicious attacks against the Jews living in German cities, murdering, forcing baptisms and causing terrible destructions.

It is a paradox that at the same time a new enlightenment developed in Germany. New inventions that were made all over Europe, made life more convenient and easier; the *Dreifelderwirtschaft* (one third of the field grew summer crops, another third grew winter crops and the last third was left uncultivated. This rotation system enabled part of the field to recover) greatly improved farming; the first German literature was established, the *Minnesänger* (minnesingers) wrote and performed their ballads, and the population increased. The first legal code of the Middle Ages, the *Sachsenspiegel*, was written between 1215 and 1235. Cities (all of them surrounded by city walls for protection) prospered through the increase of trade, the **Hanse** (Hanseatic League), an alliance of traders, turned the whole North and Baltic See area into a united center of business. It is also the time of impressive, domineering castles, where the noble life was demonstrated. It was the beginning of a prosperous era.

Many impressive architectural constructions from this time can be visited all over Germany, mainly cathedrals and castles:
• The most important castles of that period are the Burgruine Münzenberg (www.muenzenberg.de/burg.html   – only in

German) and the Wartburg in Eisenach (www.wartburg-eisenach.de – also in English)
- Just as famous are several castles along the Rhine river www.jhelbach.de/rheintal/burgen.htm (only in German) and www.loreleyvalley.com (English)
- Zisterzienserabtei Maulbronn close to Vaihingen, a convent from the Middle Ages in very good condition (www.maulbronn.de – also in English)
- Trier, Köln and Lübeck still feature many buildings and mementoes from those times
- Kaiserpfalz Gelnhausen (www.schloesser-hessen.de/54.html – only in German) and Kaiserpfalz Goslar (www.goslar.de – also in English)
- Cathedrals in Mainz (www.mainz.de – also in English) and Worms (www.wormser-dom.de – only in German)
- The town of Quedlinburg, a most important town in those years (www.quedlinburg.de – also in English)

d. The Habsburg Family and the Late Middle Ages (1273 – 1490)

The Habsburgs were one of the most important families in southwest Germany by the 13th century. Their power was manifested when Rudolf von Habsburg was made German king in 1273, after a period of unrest of more than twenty years following the death of the last German king in 1250. **Rudolf I.**, as he was called from then on, led Germany into a new heyday. Universities were founded and blossomed, the **Gothic style** became popular in Germany, especially evident in the construction of new cathedrals. Piety still had a strong influence on life in general. On the other hand, torture and severe punishments were applied more and more often and warfare entered a new phase of brutality through the use of firearms.

Cities flourished and trade continued to increase, and as more and more people flooded the cities, the space of which was limited by city walls, they became crowded and almost burst with the fill of buildings. This, no doubt, facilitated the spreading of **the plague**, which began to get Europe into its deadly grip by 1347, reaching Germany around 1350, and yet again in 1356. Further outbreaks followed until the end of the

14th century.

The late 14th century brought forth the most famous German pirate, **Klaus Störtebeker**, who successfully attacked many of the fully loaded trade ships coming to Hamburg and therefore accumulated impressive riches. He was caught in 1400 and executed in 1401. Due to his success, his riches and his execution, he became almost a legend, several adventurous tales revolved around him. In 1982, he even got his own statue in Hamburg – on the spot where he was beheaded more than 500 years before.

The middle of the 15th century brought mankind another large step towards education and enlightenment, as **Johannes Gutenberg** developed the technique of printing books. Until then, books were copied in handwriting, mainly by monks. Now the foundation for a more extensive production of books had been set.

Places and attractions where you can get an impression of Gothic architecture and learn more about the Late Middle Ages are:

- Elisabethkirche Marburg (www.elisabethkirche.de – only in German)
- Marienkirche Trier (www.trier.de – also in English)
- Cologne Cathedral (www.koelner-dom.de – also in English)
- Rothenburg o.d. Tauber, a beautiful town which illustrates beautifully what a town in the Late Middle Ages looked like (www.rothenburg.de – also in English)
- Mainz, the Gutenberg city, where museums and other attractions inform visitors about the art of book printing (www.mainz.de – also in English, www.gutenberg.de – also in English)

e. The Renaissance, the 30 Years' War and its Consequences (1490 – 1701)

The 16th and 17th century was an exciting period. Education and art flourished continuously. Famous painters dominated the scenes, like **Albrecht Dürer, Lukas Cranach** or **Tilman Riemenschneider**. The German economy grew and the era of early capitalism began. Buying things with money instead of just exchanging goods became more popular.

For some time, Germany had looked like a patchwork blanket – numerous little duchies, archbishoprics, kingdoms, principalities or counties had contributed to establishing the country. This was not to change for several centuries, posing difficulties for further economic development or political stability.

Although the Renaissance period brought so many positive developments, at the same time one of the most horrible "legal" crimes took place – the **witch hunt**. It started around 1450 and continued until the early 18th century, the climax being between 1560 – 1600 and 1650 – 1670, resulting in the death of more than 100,000 innocent people. The hysteria of the inquisition mounded into the hysteria of the witch-hunt. In the early 14th century, Pope Johannes XXII already listed the signs of witchcraft. In 1487, a legal code for the witch hunt was formulated, called the Hexenhammer, which stipulated the characteristics of a witch, describing the crimes witches committed and the kind of torture that should be applied in order to get a confession. This book had twenty-nine new editions between 1487 and 1669. Further books verified the legalization of the witch hunt. If a person was accused of being a witch, there was usually no escape, as the abominable torture methods forced most of the victims to confess whatever was demanded. Witches generally were executed. It was easy to accuse a witch and many people doubtlessly used this method to get rid of disagreeable neighbors or family members or simply people whose behavior wasn't within the norm. Midwives were in extreme danger of being accused of witchery, as they had access to children who hadn't been baptized yet and were therefore considered easy prey for witches and the devil. The last German execution of a witch took place as late as 1775.

A time of religious unrest started in 1517, when **Martin Luther** began the reformation. The reformation quickly found followers and resulted in a dispute about the true belief. As a result, the Augsburger Religionsfrieden (Augsburg Religious Peace Treaty) was put into force in 1555, announcing that everyone had the right to choose his own faith without having to fear any negative consequences. Although it was a noble step, it didn't end the religious conflicts in Germany completely. In fact, the religious conflicts in all of Europe eventually turned into an immense catastrophe – the **Thirty Years' War**. The war was actually a series of smaller battles among several European countries that took place over a period of thirty years and caused scenes of incredible destruction. None of the nations participating in this war ever managed to get the upper hand and so finally peace agreements were initiated and found their conclusion in the city of Münster with the *Westfälische Frieden* (Westphalian Peace Treaty) in 1648.

The consequences of the Thirty Years' War were numerous and catastrophic. Wide regions of Germany were completely destroyed and in the severely affected areas the population had been reduced by 50% or more. Peasants were totally impoverished as their fields had been completely demolished. This encouraged some members of the nobility to buy large stretches of land and to force the indebted peasants into serfdom. Production plants had been destroyed and there were not enough workers to speedily resume production. Most of the large trading companies and families were ruined. The Medieval structures were destroyed for ever. Germany was ready for a new epoch. It was already reflected in the new architectural style of baroque that commenced in the years following the *Westfälische Friede*. The end of the 17th century saw the construction of many magnificent palaces of a hitherto unknown splendor.

Many buildings and cities still show signs of those years of change:
- Augsburg (www.augsburg.de – also in English), Wittenberg (www.wittenberg.de – also in English) and Eisleben (www.lutherstadt-eisleben.de – also in English) – the city of the Augsburger Religionsfrieden and the towns where Martin Luther lived give a good impression of the Reformation period
- For Renaissance architecture, visit the Hämelschenburg a.d. Weser (www.schloss-haemelschenburg.de – only in German) or the Frankfurt Cathedral (www.dom-frankfurt.de – only in German)

- Donauwörth – beautifully kept town with many Renaissance buildings (www.donauwoerth.de – also in English)
- Münster, the location of the Westfälische Frieden with a well-preserved historical town center. The room in which the Westfälische Frieden was concluded (*Friedenssaal*) can be visited in the town hall (www.muenster.de – also in English)
- Some torture museums (*Foltermuseum*) tell you about the law system in those days and about the witch hunts. There are in several cities, among them Rüdesheim (www.foltermuseum.com – also in English) or Rothenburg (www.kriminalmuseum.rothenburg.de – also in English)
- Good examples of the new baroque architecture are the castles of
  o Nymphenburg in München / Munich (www.schloss-nymphenburg.de – also in English)
  o Würzburg (www.residenz-wuerzburg.de – also in English)
  o Fulda (www.schloss-fasanerie.de – also in English)
  o Karlsruhe (www.landesmuseum.de – also in English)
  o Mannheim (www.schloss-mannheim.de – also in English)
  o Kassel-Wilhelmshöhe (www.wilhelmshoehe.de – only in German)
  o Brühl (www.schlossbruehl.de – also in English)
  o Bamberg (www.schloesser.bayern.de/englisch/palace/objects/seehof.htm – English)
  o Bruchsal (www.schloss-bruchsal.de – also in English)

f. Preußen (Prussia) – A New Power (1701 – 1815)

In 1701, the up to that time relatively unimpressive area of Preußen (Prussia) in Eastern Germany made the first step into becoming one of the most impressive powers within Germany, when Friedrich III from Brandenburg crowned himself King Friedrich I of Preußen. Soon, the name of Preußen didn't only apply to the small kingdom on the Baltic Coast but to all lands belonging to the Hohenzollern, the family of Friedrich I. Berlin in Brandenburg became the new residence for the kings of Preußen and experienced a time of frenzied building activities. The Berlin City Castle, soon to be called Charlottenburg, was vastly expanded after the model of Versailles.

In 1713, Friedrich I died and his son Friedrich Wilhelm I, who would soon get the nickname "soldier king" (*Soldatenkönig*) took over the reign of Preußen. Considering his nickname it comes as no surprise to hear that his main focus was the military, even though it should be mentioned that he also introduced compulsory education. The army became the most important institution of Preußen, the largest part of tax revenue was spent for its upkeep. It was the beginning of the domination of uniforms in Preußen, which would never cease until the end of the kingdom in 1918. In spite of the large army expenses, Friedrich Wilhelm I was a thrifty king and managed to do what most governments envy highly – avoid any state debts whatsoever and even amassing an impressive state treasure.

When he died in 1740, his son Friedrich II (later called **Friedrich der Große** / Friedrich the Great or less respectfully: "*Der Alte Fritz*" / "Old Fritz") took over a well-sorted, highly-known and prosperous Preußen. He didn't lose any time to expand and just a few months after taking over the reign challenged Austria (at that time reigned by the famous empress Maria Theresia) and marched into Schlesien (Silesia). After two wars in Silesia against Austria (1740 – 1742 and 1744 – 1745), Preußen had taken over Silesia and considerably expanded its territory, but at high financial cost.

Yet another war, the Seven Years' War (*Siebenjähriger Krieg*) took place between 1756 – 1763, when Friedrich der Große witnessed Russia, France and Austria forming alliances against Preußen, arming themselves and obviously preparing for war. Friedrich der Große didn't wait to see what they would do, but marched into Sachsen (Saxonia), which resulted in Sweden joining the alliance against Preußen. Preußen, facing allied enemies, suffered many military defeats during the ensuing war. Additionally, the country itself was greatly burdened with the growing discontent of the people, the weakening of its soldiers and growing financial difficulties. Just as the situation seemed hopeless, Tsarina Elisabeth of Russia died and was succeeded by her son Peter III, who had a weak spot for Preußen. He left the alliance and made a peace treaty with Preußen. Preußen came out of the Seven-Years

War relatively unscathed as it could keep Silesia and secured its position as an important European power. Friedrich der Große did everything to rebuild his country swiftly and gave generous help to his people. After difficult years and the growing discontent of the people, Preußen slowly recovered and the king became increasingly popular.

Preußen prospered again in the course of the remaining half of the 18th century. Berlin resumed building further castles and monuments, including Sanssouci Castle and the Brandenburger Tor. The economy flourished, religious tolerance became prevalent and the judicature maked great steps towards a better organization and enlightenment. A new and – for those times – very modern general legal code was published in 1794, the *"Allgemeine Preußische Landrecht"*.

Not only Preußen, but all of Germany witnessed an impressive and unsurpassed blossoming of culture. The greatest minds of Germany excelled in the arts, the music was dominated by **Johann Sebastian Bach, Joseph Haydn** and **Ludwig van Beethoven** and literature saw geniuses as **Gotthold Ephraim Lessing, Johann Gottfried Herder, Friedrich Schiller** and of course **Johann Wolfgang von Goethe**, all of them creating works of art that survived the centuries until today. The absolute cultural center in those years was the small and politically absolutely unimportant town of **Weimar** in the duchy Sachsen-Weimar. The duchess Anna Amalie and her son Karl August made successful efforts to attract Germany's cultural elite to move to Weimar. Goethe lived in Weimar for close to sixty years of his long fruitful life. The Court Theater of Weimar (for many years under the direction of Goethe) was the location of the premieres of several plays written by Goethe and Schiller.

Larger parts of the German population than ever before gained access to education and culture, the schools and universities worked at a high level, people discovered their interest in literature and theater, which hitherto had been the exclusive domain of the nobility, and literary circles blossomed all over the country. Rich society ladies opened their parlors to the political and literary minds and the so-called *"Bildungsbürgertum"* (educated middle classes) flourished.

In 1804 clouds started forming when Napoleon Bonaparte crowned himself the Emperor of France. Napoleon started a swift conquest of Europe. He was admired by many Southern German rulers who saw him as a symbol for progress. Sixteen of these German rulers – all from the South of Germany – left the German Empire and founded the *Rheinbund* (Rhine federation) in 1806. This clear statement against the Empire marked the end for the *Römische Reich Deutscher Nation*, which started about thousand years before under Karl der Große (see page 48). The German Emperor Franz I had to resign. Things happened quickly then. Napoleon marched into Germany, defeated the Preußen armies in Jena and Auerstedt and on October 27, 1806, Napoleon entered Berlin, which surrendered without a battle. It was a fatal blow to the kingdom of Preußen.

However, Napoleon's time of glory didn't last long. 1812 saw his immense defeat in Russia, which encouraged the Preußen people to organize themselves against the French Emperor. An alliance was formed with Russia in early 1813, Austria joined it soon after. On October 16, 1813, in the *Völkerschlacht* close to Leipzig, Russian, Austrian and Preußen military joined together in a monumental fight against Napoleon, resulting in a total defeat of the French. By the end of 1813, Germany was freed from French occupation.

Napoleon had to agree to the Paris peace treaty in 1814 and even though he didn't give up his ambitious plans, the battle in Waterloo in 1815 meant the end of Napoleon.

Many of the impressive castles and buildings from the early years of Preußen can still be seen in Berlin and several other places document the rise of Preußen and the battle against Napoleon:
- Castle Charlottenburg in Berlin, the residence of the Preußen Royal Family (www.spsg.de – also in English)
- Castle Sanssouci, Potsdam, another residence of the Preußen Royal Family (www.sanssouci-sightseeing.de – only in German or: www.aviewoncities.com/berlin/sanssoucipark.htm – English)
- Brandenburger Tor, the famous Brandenburg Gate, one of Berlin's symbols. It was built in the late 18th century as the

first Greek Revival construction (www.aviewoncities.com/berlin/brandenburgertor.htm – English)
- Weimar, the beautiful little town where Goethe, Schiller and some other main contributors to German culture lived. (www.weimar.de – also in English)
- Völkerschlachtdenkmal Leipzig, the memorial of the victory over Napoleon in 1813 (www.voelkerschlachtdenkmal.de – only in German)
- Museum 1806 in Cospeda by Jena, the museum about the 1806 battle against Napoleon at Jena-Auerstedt (www.jena1806.de – only in German)
- Bachhaus in Eisenach, a beautiful historic building that was the first museum to be dedicated to Johann Sebastian Bach (www.bachhaus.de – also in English)

g. The Wiener Kongreß and the Fight for German Unity (1815 – 1871)

Napoleon changed everything, national structures were not as before and Europe urgently needed "sorting out". The heads of the European countries met in Vienna to re-organize Europe. The so-called *Wiener Kongreß* (Vienna Convention) ended in 1815. The result? The continent now had five main powers (Austria, England, France, Germany and Russia) whereby the Kingdom of Poland became part of Russia, England acquired several islands including Malta and Helgoland, and Preußen gained territory in the west and within Sachsen (Saxonia). Switzerland received a new constitution and its eternal neutrality was acknowledged, and the United Kingdom of the Netherlands was founded. Unfortunately, several changes were also made that sewed the seed for future riots, conflicts and battles in the coming centuries; for example, unnatural borders were established by dividing and re-uniting the population against their will.

The former *Römische Reich Deutscher Nation* was now substituted by the **Deutsche Bund** (German Federation), which far from being a united Germany just constitutes a loose federation of duchies and independent cities with one government organ – the *Bundestag* in Frankfurt, where representatives from all members of the German Federation met. As the Deutsche Bund also included Hannover (under the reign of the English king), Luxemburg (under the reign of the Dutch king) and Holstein (under the reign of the Danish king), as well as parts of Preußen and Austria, rulers from different countries were brought together, which made it impossible to turn the *Deutsche Bund* into a national and united German state.

As a result, many Germans were disappointed, as their expectations had not been fulfilled. They reacted in two different ways. A majority of the population turned their backs on politics and focused more on their private lives, enjoying their homes and families more and cultivating friendships. This period, with its idealization of family life and its emphasis on beautiful and comfortable homes was called **Biedermeier.** The furniture from this period is highly elegant, very sought after today and consequently extremely expensive.

The other disappointed group however, mainly German students, did not dream of accepting the new situation. They wanted to fight for a united Germany, if necessary by means of a revolution. In 1817, several hundred students went to the Wartburg for the *Wartburgfest* (Wartburg festival). Officially, the reason for the *Wartburgfest* was the 300th anniversary of the reformation as well as the commemoration of the Völkerschlacht, which basically ended Napoleon's grip on Europe. Instead, the occasion was used for passionate speeches in favour of German unity, rejecting the results of the Wiener Kongreß. The government became nervous when symbols standing for the repression were burned. A convention in Karlsbad (it's now a Czech town, the Czech name is Karlovy Vary) was held after further unrest, where the heads of several German duchies met and agreed on the *Karlsbader Beschlüsse* (Karlsbad Decisions). These introduced censorship and limited students'/professors' rights to a great extent, enabling the secret police to arrest and imprison critics of the system. Preußen was extremely vehement in fighting any rebellious subjects. Many Germans had no choice but to leave the country.

Still, amidst this repressive police state, education and arts flourished. Goethe was still active in Weimar and new composers like **Felix Mendelssohn-Bartholdy, Franz Schubert** or **Robert Schumann** added to the culture and Ludwig van

Beethoven's famous Ninth Symphony premiered in 1824 in Vienna. The Greek Revival architectural style became increasingly popular and the Bildungsbürgertum continued its culturally inspired social life. The Germans seemed to be sufficiently subdued. However, all changed in 1830.

1830 was the year of yet another French revolution, a people's successful fight for freedom. It inspired the Germans and pulled them from their political lethargy. Tens of thousands of people gathered at the Hambacher Castle in 1832 to demonstrate for democracy and unity. The rulers reacted mercilessly and the political suppression became even stronger and fiercer. However, this time the Germans would not give up that easily. The political unrest smoldered until it exploded again in 1848.

The years in between saw further changes. Germany became a modern industrial state, with the **first German railway train** starting to run in 1835 and advances in medicine and hygiene resulting in an amazing growth of the population. Unfortunately, this went ahead with meager harvests and lower wages as there was not enough employment for everyone. Large parts of the population became incredibly poor which caused further turbulences.

It was France again that influenced Europe with a **revolution in 1848**. This time the revolutionary mood conquered Germany in no time. The Germans tried something new, they went on the streets, mainly in Vienna and Berlin. Berlin saw violent fights between the revolutionists and the king's army and finally a first step was made towards democracy – a national assembly of elected representatives from all states of the *Deutsche Bund* met in the **Frankfurt Paulskirche** (Paul's church) on May 18, 1848, in order to formulate a constitution. They met until March 28, 1849 when the new constitution was finally announced. The plan was to turn Germany into a constitutional monarchy and so the Preußen king Friedrich Wilhelm IV was approached by the national assembly on April 3, 1849. They offered him the position of the German Emperor, elected by the German people. However, while the national assembly was discussing the German constitution, Preußen and Austria had dealt with the revolutionaries their own way and were in a secure position again, troops had occupied Berlin and the Preußen king had introduced a Preußen Constitution, which was already a sign that Preußen didn't want a national German unity. Friedrich Wilhelm IV therefore didn't care to receive a crown from the hands of his people and so he refused both the crown and the national constitution. That brought a quick end to both the national assembly and any attempts of unity. The revolution was over.

In 1862, a man named **Otto von Bismarck** (1815 – 1898) was elected Preußen's Prime Minister. He would shape German politics for the next twenty-eight years leading Preußen to become the main power in Germany. He was deeply conservative, shunned everything that seemed to be liberal and quickly announced that he wanted to expand Preußen's lands and power, if necessary, with military force. True to his word, he quickly moved to attack Preußen's biggest rival – Austria. The war against Austria began in 1866 and ended after just a few months with a clear victory of the Preußen troops in the **battle of Königgrätz** (today it's a Czech town called Hradec Králové) on July 3, 1866. Bismarck reached his goal – Austria was no longer a part of Germany. The Deutsche Bund was dissolved and in 1867 Preußen and several German states north of the Main formed the ***Norddeutsche Bund*** (Northern German Federation) with Preußen as the strongest and most important power. The times of sharing the supremacy in Germany with Austria were over.

Bismarck was going in the right direction and he didn't wait long before taking the next step. In 1870, Germany and France were at war with each other. Germany quickly demonstrated its strength and decided the war to its advantage in the battle of Sedan (the anniversary of which was then commemorated in Germany for many decades following) on September 1, 1870. This victory was to be the foundation for a united German Empire.

Several landmarks and worthy sights from those years are:
• Wartburg in Eisenach, site of the Wartburgfest in 1817 (www.wartburg-eisenach.de – also in English)
• Paulskirche in Frankfurt, the site where the first German constitution was drafted in 1848. (http://altfrankfurt.com/

Kirchen/Paulskirche/ - also in English)
- Museum Knoblauchhaus in Berlin, a town mansion from the 18th century, it has an exhibition about "Living in the Biedermeier times" where you can see how houses were furnished in the Biedermeier period (www.stadtmuseum.de/knoblauchhaus - also in English)
- The Bismarck-Route is a driving tour that takes you to places that played a role in the life of Otto von Bismarck and his family (www.altmarktourismus.de/pages/bismarck_route.html – only in German or contact: info@altmarktourismus.de for further information)

h. The German Empire (1871 – 1918)

During the French-German War, Bismarck had already started to convince the rulers of the southern German states to unite with the Norddeutsche Bund, thereby forming one German Empire with the Preußen king as its emperor. In the end he succeeded, with the consequence that he took great influence in financial matters of the southern states.

After the French defeat, the Germans used the large Mirror Hall of the Versailles Castle for the **crowning ceremony** of the new German emperor, **Wilhelm I.** The new German Empire now covered the area of today's Germany as well as large areas in the east – Eastern Prussia, Silesia and Pomerania – and Alsace and Lothringen in the west, which France lost to Germany during the war. The empire now was a vast and powerful country and the German people revelled in their triumph. Almost sixty years after the *Wiener Kongreß* Germany was finally one country with a constitutional monarchy. A new sense of national pride emerged. As France had been forced to pay an extremely high reparation to Germany through the peace treaty, the country felt prosperous with its already flourishing economy and the people had the impression of sharing this new established wealth.

It was the beginning of the *Gründerjahre* (Founding Years), when many new companies were founded and when the people who could afford it indulged in parties, expensive clothes and excessive spending. For the following two years, one had the impression that most of Germany was celebrating one big party. The financial panic that hit the world in 1873 brought this joyful life to an abrupt end, but it was only a temporary setback and Germany saw a new architectural era soon afterwards – copying several other styles – with one main purpose – to show affluence. Rich families built large and impressive villas to demonstrate their wealth, not forgetting clothes fashion as an additional reflection of evident wealth. Berlin, the German capital, was the "big spender" *par excellence*, especially the German Court developed an attitude of pretentiousness. The rail network was extended and large industrial cities grew rapidly. However, the population grew as well and because more and more people rushed into the cities to search for jobs, affordable housing was increasingly difficult to find. While the palatial mansions of the rich dominated large areas of the cities, the number of homeless people increased steadily. In the larger cities many working class families lived in one single room and were even forced to take in lodgers so that they were able to afford the rent.

The deplorable situation of the workers enabled the unions and the Social Democratic Party of Germany to flourish, which not only made the government highly nervous, but also the conservative Bismarck. The state reverted to measures it had already used in previous decades – suppression and oppression. As a kind of preventative measure, the laws on which the **welfare state** (see page 86) was to be established were ratified in the 1880s, to give German workers the impression that the Empire was taking care of them.

Bismarck's foreign policy was extremely complicated and consisted of several alliances with other countries to ensure peace. As long as Bismarck was alive to preside over the different alliances and contracts, things worked out quite well, although that would change in the following century.

The first German Emperor, Wilhelm I, died on March 9, 1888 at the respectable age of 91. His son and successor, **Friedrich III**, was already terminally ill with cancer when he became Emperor. He only reigned for 99 days and then died on June 15, 1888 at the age of 56. His son, **Wilhelm II** (1859 – 1941), became the new – and last – Emperor of the German Empire. In the short span of three months, Germany had had three emperors.

Wilhelm II was more tolerant towards the workers and liberals and followed a new political route, which didn't go well with Bismarck. Bismarck observed this development for two years, but then, disillusioned, resigned his post in 1890, much to the pleasure of Wilhelm II, who preferred making decisions on his own.

New inventions like cars, electricity, the cinema or flying combined with more social security for workers made **Wilhelminian Germany** a pleasant place to live. Once again culture blossomed, the Jugendstil was popular, Germany became the European center of expressionism. Composers like **Richard Wagner** and writers like **Theodor Fontane, Gerhart Hauptmann, Rainer Maria Rilke** and the **Mann brothers Heinrich and Thomas** dominated the scene. Many medical and scientific discoveries (virus that causes tuberculosis, chemotherapy, x-rays, theory of relativity) were made in Germany as well, and a substantial number of **nobel prizes** went to the German Empire during this period.

Wilhelm II was enthused about anything military, he always liked to present himself as being very much of a soldier. The already dominant army attained even more significance resulting in a new craze for uniforms in the country. You were only somebody if you wore a uniform. Carl Zuckmayer wrote a play (*"Der Hauptmann von Köpenick"*) in 1931 based on a true story that took place in Wilhelminian Berlin in 1906. An unemployed ex-convict, Wilhelm Voigt, desperately tried to acquire the necessary official documents in order to take up work and find somewhere to live, but he failed completely due to the inflexible bureaucracy. He managed to get hold of a military uniform, put it on and in next to no time took over power in the town hall of the Berlin district of Köpenick. The effect of wearing a uniform was amazing. Everybody regarded him as a highly powerful individual and followed his orders without question. He went as far as to have the mayor of Köpenick arrested. The story and the play that made it famous illustrate the significance of wearing a uniform very clearly.

Wilhelm II's foreign politics reflected his passion for the military. The German Empire built up a large and powerful military fleet, which worried the other European countries. Wilhelm II also decided that it was time for the empire to acquire its share of colonies, which he did in Africa and Asia. Because of his lack of diplomacy and tact, the emperor became quite unpopular in Europe; his foreign policy combined with his growing power caused the neighboring countries to feel uneasy resulting in a decline of good relations with France, Russia and England.

At the beginning of the **First World War**, the German population was enthusiastic, but that changed quickly as the German Empire experienced one military defeat after the other. By 1918, the Germans were tired of the war and shocked at the immense losses they had suffered. The beginning of November 1918 saw strikes and riots that soon spread over the whole country to quickly develop into a full-blown **revolution**. The people demanded the Emperor's resignation, which Wilhelm II complied to on November 9, 1918 before going into exile in the Netherlands. Germany became a republic.

Many mansions of the Gründerzeit still exist, mainly in Berlin. The beautiful city of Leipzig also has a large area of Gründerzeit houses (Waldstraßenviertel). Many other monuments are reminders of the final years of the German Empire:

- Niederwald Denkmal close to Rüdesheim – this large statue of Germania holding the Imperial crown in her right and the Imperial sword in her left hand commemorates the founding of the German Empire (www.niederwalddenkmal.de – also in English)
- Villa Hügel – this Essen mansion was build by the industrial giant Alfred Krupp and is a good example of a Gründerzeit home (www.villahuegel.de – also in English)
- Reichstag, the seat of the German parliament, built at the end of the 19th century (www.bundestag.de/besucher – also in English)
- Berlin Cathedral, finished in 1905 (though there have been other cathedral buildings on this site for several hundred years before) is a good example of the grand Wilhelminian building style (www.berliner-dom.de – also in English)
- Festspielhaus Bayreuth, the location of the famous Bayreuther Festspiele (Bayreuth Opera Festivals), built 1872 – 1875 according to Richard Wagner's ideas

(www.bayreuther-festspiele.de – also in English)
*   The Zeppelinmuseum Friedrichshafen at Lake Constance, in which the history and development of the zeppelin is described (www.zeppelin-museum.de – also in English)

i. The Way into World War II and the Destruction of Germany (1918 – 1945)

The new republic didn't get off to a very good start. The peace treaty ending World War I was signed in June 1919 (the armistice had been on November 11, 1918) in the Mirror Hall of Versailles – the same room that had been the scene of the proclamation of the first German emperor 48 years previously. The contents of the peace treaty shocked and humiliated a discouraged and impoverished Germany. Germany was acclaimed solely responsible for starting the war and was condemned to pay extremely high reparations as well as losing large regions of its empire.

On August 11, 1919, Germany's new constitution was announced. As it had been formulated in the small town of Weimar, the new republic was named *Weimarer Republik*. The constitution was motivated by the best intentions, but in the following years it proved incapable of providing a basis for a stable government. The Weimarer Republik soon suffered under innumerous riots, assassinations, and constant changes of governments. Right-wing groups, who didn't care for a republic under the Social Democratic Party, organized several coup d'états, the most famous of which were the *Kapp-Putsch* of 1920 and the *Hitler-Putsch* of 1923. In 1922, the German currency lost its value and by 1923 Germany was in the middle of a massive inflation, which led to the introduction of a new currency, the *Rentenmark*. The German people possessed bills with astronomical numbers printed on them which were worthless. My grandfather remembers that the children were given those bills to play with.

The relative stability of the **Rentenmark** ensured the young republic a more peaceful period. The **Dawes Plan** was introduced in 1924 and relieved Germany somewhat of the severity of reparations. Relations with other countries slowly improved and in 1926 Germany became a member of the *Völkerbund*, an international association that devoted itself to maintaining peace. The country was no longer completely isolated. Further contracts and agreements secured a better European understanding.

Slowly but steadily the German economy recovered, making way for the "Golden Twenties". Established and new artists like **Gerhart Hauptmann, Thomas and Heinrich Mann, Franz Werfel, Otto Dix** or **Erich Kästner** contributed to the cultural life. Radio and sound film were innovations in the world of entertainment. A new generation of modern artists developed and the streamline Bauhaus architecture became popular. Large industrial families formed the new upper class, replacing the nobility in this prominent position.

But the end of the "Golden Twenties" drew near. The **financial panic of 1929** shattered the world. Unemployment and poverty hit the just recovered Weimarer Republik, accompanied by new strikes and riots. The **National Socialist Party of Germany (NSDAP)** gained increasing popularity because of its full-mouthed promises of ending unemployment and challenging the humiliating conditions of the Versailles Peace Treaty. Within a few years, the NSDAP became so strong that the government had no choice but to make the party leader, **Adolf Hitler** (1889 – 1945), the new Reichskanzler and thereby the head of the country. Although unknown at the time, Germany's days as a republic were numbered as of January 30, 1933.

Hitler lost no time in securing total power "legally", which the weak Weimar Constitution enabled him to do. Within a few months free elections were abolished, all other political parties were forbidden and countless people were arrested and interned or killed. The merciless persecution of everyone considered to oppose the regime was continued until the end of Hitler's rule in 1945. Children and adults were forced into organized groups like the *Hitlerjugend* (Hitler Youth), the *Bund Deutscher Mädel* (League of German girls, basically the female *Hitlerjugend*) or the *Reichsarbeitsdienst* (Reich Labour Service). Every form of individuality was suppressed. The cultural elite was divided, some collaborate with the new regime, others went into exile. Actions against the Jews began immediately, but proceeded slowly step by step, gradually worsening until they culminated in the *Reichskristallnacht* on

November 9, 1938 followed by the systematic deportation and killing of millions of Jews. Step by step, Germany moved in the direction of war and destruction. **World War II** began on September 1, 1939, when German troops invaded Poland. After a period of initial military successes resulted in the occupation of most of the European continent, the war ended with the total annihilation of Germany through the allied forces. Hitler committed suicide on April 30, 1945 and on May 8 of the same year, the war was over and Germany a field of ruins.

- If you want to learn more about the Bauhaus culture, you can visit Bauhaus museums in Berlin (www.bauhaus.de – also in English) or Weimar (https://www.klassik-stiftung.de/einrichtungen/museen/bauhaus-museum-weimar – also in English)
- The House of the infamous Wannsee Conference (where the murder of the Jews was officially agreed upon) is now a memorial and educational center – www.ghwk.de (also in English)
- Some of the Nazi concentration camps are now memorials, like Buchenwald (www.buchenwald.de – also in English) or Dachau (www-kz-gedenkstaette-dachau.de – also in English)
- Tower of the Kaiser-Wilhelm-Gedächtniskirche, Berlin – this tower is the only part left of this church after Berlin was bombed. The church was rebuilt in modern style and the tower has been left standing as a memorial to the bombings of Word War II (www.gedaechtniskirche-berlin.de – also in English)

j. **The Division and Reunification of Germany; Germany Today (1945 –)**

World War II left Germany in a state of desolution and despair. Millions of people were driven away from their homes. Many **refugee treks** were organized in the eastern regions of what had been the German Empire (East Prussia, Silesia or Pomerania) in January 1945, struggling their way westward during the icy, cold winter. Many people died of hunger and exhaustion on the way, but many also arrived in the western part of Germany. The country was now full of refugees and people who had lost their homes in the bombings. As most areas only consisted of ruins, people settled in these ruins as well as they could, or they were put in large refugee camps. Many families had been separated and family members were scattered all over the country. They left messages in chalk on ruin walls of their whereabouts for other family members to read in case one or the other turned up. Many men were still prisoners of war in camps far away in the countries of the allies for several years after 1945.

In July 1945, the famous **Potsdam Conference** with Churchill/Atlee, Truman and Stalin took place. The result of this meeting was the Potsdam Agreement which set the rules to be applied in occupied Germany: Denazification, bringing war criminals to court, complete disarmament and demilitarization, democratization, designating a governmental power in each of the occupied zones (under either the Americans, the French, the British or the Russians), industrial control and dismantling of industrial plants through the occupying powers. Germany lost large regions of land in the east – Pomerania, Eastern Prussia and Silesia became parts of Poland and Russia. Reparations also had to be paid. German civilians who still lived in Poland, the Czech Republic and Hungary had to be transported to Germany in an "orderly and humane" fashion (which was seldom the case). Differences between Russia and the western allies were already noticeable during the Potsdam Conference and led to heated debates regarding the contents of the agreement. Basically, the Potsdam Conference marked the beginning of the **Cold War**.

Denazification began immediately – every German citizen over the age of 18 had to fill out a questionnaire with 131 questions covering personal data, education, religious and political involvement and many other issues. After the questionnaire was evaluated, the individual was placed in one of five categories – "principal culprit" (hauptschuldig), "incriminated" (belastet), "less incriminated" (minderbelastet), "hanger-on" (Mitläufer) or "exonerated" (entlastet). Individuals, known to have opposed the Nazi regime or who had suffered under the regime, were requested by others to provide documents confirming the anti-Nazi attitude of the requester. These documents were supposed to insinuate that this individual was less incriminated. They were half-jokingly called "Persilschein" (Persil certificate) as they "cleaned" people of the suspicion of having been a Nazi – just like the washing detergent "Persil" removed dirt from clothes. Nevertheless, the questionnaires and categorizing was soon abandoned, as it was recognized they were not helpful in finding the really big war criminals.

Many members of the Nazi elite had been arrested, and on November 20, 1945, the famous trial against war criminals took place – the **Nürnberger Prozess**. It lasted until October 1, 1946 and ended with twelve death sentences and seven prison sentences as well as three acquittals. The death sentences were executed on the morning of October 1, 1946. The only one to escape his execution was **Hermann Göring**, who committed suicide the previous night. The men with prison sentences were taken to the prison in Berlin Spandau. During the following decades one after the other was released after serving their sentences, the odd one was released prematurely for health reasons. Between late 1966 and 1987 there was only one prisoner left in Spandau – **Rudolf Heß**, who had been sentenced to life. He died in prison on August 17, 1987 at the age of ninety-three.

Germany showed verve and stamina in rebuilding and reorganizing the country. As early as late 1945 the first German political parties were re-founded and the population had already started clearing away the rubble and ruins from the countless bombardments everywhere. This work was mainly carried out by women as many men had been killed during the war, were missing or were kept as prisoners of war. These women have earned their place in history under the name "**Trümmerfrauen**" – rubble women.

The late 1940s were extremely hard. People starved or froze to death (especially in the severe winter of 1946/47), the survivors tried to find their missing relatives and were deeply traumatized by the events of the previous years. For many years after the war – decades in fact, the subject of the Nazi epoch was taboo. The US foreign minister, Marshall helped build up a new Germany with the famous "**Marshall Plan**" in 1948. It helped to organize and revive Germany's economy as part of the "European Recovery Program". The introduction of a new currency – the **Deutschmark** – in the western occupation zones 1948 brought further stability and the end of ration cards. Suddenly, all kind of goods were available to everyone again and the road was clear for the so-called *Wirtschaftswunder* (economic miracle).

However, these new developments did not extend to the eastern part of Germany, which was under Russian occupation. The former Nazi concentration camps and prisons located in the Russian zone were now being filled with so-called suspected opponents of the Russian occupation – even completely innocent people. The book "*Die Schleife an Stalins Bart*" by Erika Riemann describes the true story of a fourteen year old girl who was imprisoned for eight years just because she drew a bow around Stalin's moustache on a portrait of him as she thought he looked so sad. – Once again, uniforms and organizations dominated daily life and again the rights of the individual were being suppressed. It didn't differ much from the years of the Nazi regime. Countless people wanted to leave East Germany and fled to the western regions, increasing the number of refugees there considerably.

In 1949 two German states were founded – the **Federal Republic of Germany** in the west and the **German Democratic Republic (GDR)** in the east. The new West German Constitution (*"Grundgesetz"*) was ratified, with the reunification of Germany as one of the highest goals. **Konrad Adenauer** (1876 - 1967) became chancellor. West Germany soon flourished in the course of the *Wirtschaftswunder*. By the middle of the 1950s most of West Germany was rebuilt – an amazing accomplishment after the estimation that it would take decades to do so. The economic high tide lasted until the middle of the 1960s and the German people enjoyed their new prosperity. They traveled abroad, mainly to Italy, bought the Volkswagen (an export-hit, which greatly helped the German economy) and fitted their homes with all the latest gadgets and trendy designs. German literature also began to flourish again, with a small group of writers who came together in 1947 and called themselves **Group 47**.

East Germany was a different story. The new state, under a socialist government (dictated by Russia), was never able to develop a well-working economy and by the time the whole system broke down in 1989, East Germany was basically bankrupt. The socialist government together with Russia had kept a strong grip on the people. **June 17, 1953** saw a national uproar in East Germany, but it was quickly and brutally crushed. Tanks just drove into the crowds of people that had gathered everywhere, causing many deaths and casualties. A new tide of refugees fled to West Germany and in 1961 East Germany consequently stopped people from leaving the country. On **August 13, 1961** Germany witnessed the construction of the **Berlin Wall**, which would separate the city for the following twenty-eight years. This was a tremendous shock to the whole population. People living in the buildings right next to the wall frantically tried to jump out of their apartment windows over the wall to the west side, soldiers tried to keep them back by force and countless people in West Berlin watched the process of their fellow Berliners being walled in in speechless horror. During the next decades many people were to be arrested or shot during their attempts to overcome the wall or cross the barbed-wire fenced border with its mined death strips, guarded watch towers and dogs, that separated East Germany from West Germany. The last person to be shot there as late as February 1989 was a twenty-year-old boy called Chris Gueffroy.

During the next decades the two German states developed in completely different ways. Only very gradually did relations between West Germany and the rest of the world become more relaxed again. In 1955 West Germany became a member of the NATO, in 1963 a contract between France and Germany was established to improve relationships and in 1965 Germany and Israel took up a diplomatic relationship. In 1970, the German chancellor, **Willy Brandt** (1913 – 1992), fell onto his knees in front of a memorial for all the Jews killed in the Warsaw Ghetto, to demonstrate that the Federal Republic recognized responsibility for the atrocities committed by the Nazis between 1933 – 1945. This symbolic gesture was the first big step towards a better understanding between Germany and Poland, which had suffered tremendously under German occupation during the war. Willy Brandt received the Nobel prize for peace in 1971. The 1970s, however, did not only see improved relationships between Germany and its former enemies, but the whole country experienced a time of escalating violence, caused by a left-wing terrorist organisation known as the "RAF" (red army fraction).

In 1989, the almost unthinkable happened. Under the reign of **Mikhail Gorbatchev**, a new spirit of freedom drifted through Russia and the Eastern European States. Whereas the East German head of state, **Erich Honecker** (1912 – 1994), proclaimed that the Berlin Wall would stand another hundred years, peaceful demonstrations in East Germany demanded freedom and democracy and the rest of Eastern Europe got ready to open up. Hungary was first, the border fence to Austria was cut open in summer of 1989 and countless East Germans who had been vacationing in Hungary took the opportunity of freedom and crossed the newly opened border. On **November 9, 1989** the Berlin wall was officially opened. Everybody rushed to Berlin and all of Germany was in an enthused party mood. The reunification was planned quickly and on October 3, 1990, Germany became a reunited country.

The last decade of the 20th century had started on a hopeful note and the joy about being one country again was overwhelming, but it dwindled quickly as economic problems and unemployment increased. An extremely positive event for the whole country was the FIFA World Cup in 2006. The World Cup took place in Germany from June 9, 2006 to July 9, 2006 and during those four weeks the world undoubtedly saw a new side of Germany. As one German commentator said on TV afterwards, even if Germany didn't win the World Cup, we felt as if we won. The world saw how enthusiastic Germans can be and for the first time, Germans were happy to display their flag. Balconies, windows, cars – the black-red-gold of the flag was everywhere to be seen and the German people experienced that there is a healthy and peaceful kind of patriotism (see also page 29 about the Germans and patriotism). A wonderful sign of integration were the balconies and cars of foreigners living in Germany – they often displayed the flag of their home country together with the German flag.

Germany's motto for the World Cup was "*Zu Gast bei Freunden*" (English version: "A Time to Make Friends") and it has often been confirmed that the Germans have lived up to this motto. Every large German city had "fan fests", where those without tickets to the matches could watch the matches on giant video walls and among many other cheering fans. Cafés and restaurants put big TV screens outside so that their guests could watch the game. The World Cup undoubtedly was an event that touched and delighted Germany.

The years since have seen a big economic crisis and recovery, the Euro crisis and Germany winning the World Cup in 2014.

As you can see from this overview, Germany has a long and exciting history, it has gone through many fundamental changes and quite often its politics have brought temporary ruin and destruction. Especially the 20th century was eventful, boasting many transformations during a normal person's life span. A great-aunt of mine who lived in East Germany, for example, experienced the following during her lifetime: Between her birth in 1911 and her death in 2000, she witnessed Imperial Germany, the Weimar Republic, the Nazi regime, World War II, Russian occupation, the founding and breaking down of the GDR and the reunification of Germany. She went through four different currencies during those years, but did not get to know the Euro, which was introduced after her death. These constant changes and uplifts have deeply formed the German culture.

- Schloß Cecilienhof, Potsdam, site of the Potsdamer Konferenz in 1945 (www.spsg.de/index.php?id=126 – also in English)
- Berlin Wall - most of the Berlin Wall has been disassembled, but a short part is still there to see, it is now covered in wall painting (www.die-berliner-mauer.de - also in English)
- A museum at the former Checkpoint Charlie, one of the checkpoints on the Berlin wall, shows an exhibit about the post-war history of Berlin and about the Berlin Wall (www.mauermuseum.de - also in English)
- An very informative exhibit about how Germans lived in the 1950s can be seen in the 50er Jahre Museum in the small (and beautiful) town of Büdingen near Frankfurt (www.50er-jahre-museum.de - only in German)

IV. Culture Shock

1. What is Culture Shock?

In my questionnaire I asked if any of the respondents had experienced a culture shock after coming to Germany. Everyone answered with a clear "yes" and even one person stated that "anyone who says they don't is a liar."

It is widely acknowledged that no international move comes without a culture shock, although of course the degree of the culture shock experienced varies. This depends on how different the culture in the destination country is from the culture in the home country, how well one is prepared for the change and what kind of support one has. Some expats deal with a culture shock quite easily while others have serious problems handling it, so that, in the worst case, they would be compelled to leave the country prematurely. However, first it is necessary to define culture shock. There is a lot of literature and information on this subject, as this an unavoidable issue when one is about to live in a foreign country.

Obviously, people experience culture shock when they are confronted with a different culture in daily life. Even in countries with a similar culture to the one in your home country you can occasionally be confronted with problems. Some may be small, hardly noticeable, but they can affect daily life. In fact, it is not unusual for people to experience a bigger culture shock in countries with a similar culture to their own, as they are then less likely to be prepared for any differences. If you move from the United States to Egypt, you expect to be confronted with many unfamiliar situations and customs, so you can prepare yourself for them – different language, different continent, different religion, different food etc. You start your life in Egypt knowing that you will encounter cultural differences and difficulties. If you move from Germany to Switzerland or Austria or from the United States to Canada, you probably don't expect life there to be all that different, as they are neighboring countries, sharing the same language and customs. You would not see any need to inform yourself about any country-related special mannerisms or characteristics, so that when you are confronted with them, you are totally taken by surprise.

Generally, a culture shock goes through four major stages, as you will be able to read in many books. Some books give these stages other names, but they basically describe the similar situations one goes through when starting a new life in a foreign country. As mentioned before, the strength of symptoms differs and not everything at every stage applies to everybody, but you can use it as a guideline.

The first stage is often called the "honeymoon stage", as you feel positive and happy, are excited about the new development in your life and about the experience ahead of you – sometimes your expectations are high and can then result in a stronger disappointment later on. Daily life has not yet set in, maybe you are in temporary living in a hotel, not having to worry about shopping or chores – it is a bit like a holiday. You might even find more similarities with your home country than you had imagined and so you consider things to be easy and wonderful.

Then, the "honeymoon" stage is over and you are confronted with daily life and the problems that come with it in a different culture. Robert Lederman, from Canada, puts it simply: "Didn't have a clue on where to find anything."

And Alice Waldron says: "Bureaucracy was more complicated and stressful than expected – small things seemed to take so long (e.g. getting a phone line put in). – I got stressed and annoyed and kept comparing things to being at home."
Her last sentence clearly indicates the second stage, the "hostility stage". You feel disoriented because the customs and values you grew up with suddenly don't always apply any more. Small things relating to social interaction, e.g. how to greet people, how to do your food shopping or knowing what subjects are suitable for small talk can now be confusing, leading to a loss of security, which in turn makes you more vulnerable. First, frustration can set in, mixed with anxiety and you suddenly realize how different and difficult life in the foreign country can be. If you have no knowledge of the host country's language when moving there, it will increase the feeling of helplessness. When my parents moved from Germany to Brussels/Belgium, my mother's French was very basic and she often mentioned that small things like food shopping or

talking to doctors had suddenly become difficult and exhausting tasks. Just after the move, she had to rely on my father for certain things, for example, when a craftsman had to be called to do some work in the house, my father either had to call the required person himself or he had to be there when this person arrived at the house to explain what needed to be repaired. My mother wasn't really able to either answer or ask any questions that might have been necessary, which made her feel extremely frustrated.

Often, ethnocentrism becomes evident at this stage, an attitude that is familiar to almost everybody to some degree and basically demonstrates how people tend to reject and disapprove of foreign cultures because they believe that their own culture is the only true one. Many people at the hostility stage of a culture shock tend to look down on the ways of their host country, comparing them with their home culture – always to the disadvantage of the host country. Everything that's different is bad and stereotypes are often gladly used to confirm this opinion. Although stereotypes often contain some truth, they are a dangerous way of looking at other nationalities. Typical stereotypes about Germans are: unfriendly, rude, humorless, strict, compulsively punctual and bureaucratic. It would be wrong to apply these attributes to all Germans and to say, for example, that all Germans are rude because you have had an unpleasant encounter with an unfriendly salesperson. This kind of generalization is just as wrong as saying that all Americans are superficial, loud and only eat fast food. I hope you will meet many friendly, humorous and relaxed Germans during your stay in Germany! To find out what stereotypes you have about Germans and which ones (in your opinion) end up being confirmed, make a list at the beginning of your stay of the German traits you consider typical and then review the list after about a year to see if your perception of the Germans has changed during that time.

I learned from the questionnaires that "unfriendliness" proved to be a big issue to almost everybody. And yes, I must admit, as a widely traveled German, I am aware that most Germans at first appear less friendly and open than people of other nations. The main reason for this in my opinion is the fact that Germans are reserved by nature and tend to be less outgoing – appear less friendly – towards strangers or people they don't know well. Some of the respondents to the questionnaire stated they could cope better with this after realizing that what they believed to be unfriendliness was in fact a normal German characteristic and was not meant to be understood as a personal affront. Bonnie Barski quickly recognized this and says: "Germans seem more reserved at first. There's a different etiquette of getting to know people. Once you know them, they're like people everywhere (....), it's just a matter of personality how each one is."

Ethnocentrism and stereotyping are dangerous when dealing with culture shock. This "hostility" stage could influence the whole future course of your stay abroad. You might end up rejecting everything in connection with your host country, withdraw to the world you know and only socialize with other expats. This kind of isolation is a constant reminder of how much you miss your home country and how much you yearn to go back. One of the expats who filled out the questionnaire was apparently still at the hostility stage at the time. She couldn't find anything positive about Germany at all and announced that she thought Germans in general were aggressive and arrogant. When asked how she coped with this she answered that she was still in the process of overcoming it by getting involved in English-speaking groups and going to her home country as often as possible. While building up a social network is a step in the right direction, her focusing on other expats and her frequent trips back home indicate that she is not really ready to leave the hostility stage behind her. One expat from the UK declared that she made a point of not socializing too much with "expat-only" organizations and social circles: "I (...) found those organizations to be full of people complaining about the country when they had often not even bothered to learn the German language, find out anything about Germany or make the attempt to adapt their way of life." She clearly recognized that these people were without doubt at the hostility stage – by isolating themselves and mingling with "their own" they were not helping each other, on the contrary, they were affirming each others' situation.

If you are an accompanying spouse without the backup of

work, you are likely to have the additional problem of feeling generally lost and isolated or lonely. Maureen Chase, who accompanied her husband to Germany from the US, says about her first months in Germany: "I also sometimes lacked direction in the beginning in the sense that I didn't know what to do the next day, or the day after that or the month after that."

Whereas the expat who comes to another country to work or study is usually integrated into a world that is in many ways similar to the one at home – office surroundings, the challenges of work and usually colleagues who speak the expat's native language – the accompanying spouse often had to give up work in the home country and also misses a loss of familiar social structures in the foreign environment, while at the same time discovering that dealing with the obstacles of daily life is now completely invincible. A simple chore like buying groceries suddenly becomes an immense challenge due to language problems or different shopping structures, so it is hard not to revert to ethnocentrism.

The expats who give up at this stage and refuse to accept the host country's culture, to learn the language or to be willing to socialize with the locals and instead prefer to mingle solely in expat circles focusing their thoughts on all the negative sides of living in that country will not only be unhappy there, but will also miss the opportunity of making many wonderful new experiences – learning a new language, exploring a different country, making interesting new friends, gaining background knowledge and understanding for a different culture, maybe even developing a whole new skill.

2. How to Overcome Culture Shock

So, if you don't want your stay in Germany to end prematurely or be overshadowed by a feeling of discomfort, it is extremely important to work on yourself and be willing to enter into the third stage of your culture shock – the adjustment stage. You have reached this stage when you acquired enough knowledge of the host country's language to get around and familiarize yourself with the local surroundings, how to handle daily chores, where to make certain purchases and how to react in certain situations. Usually, you reach this adjustment stage if you are able and willing to accept and understand that a different culture is not automatically less superior than the culture of your home country. As Sarah Happel puts it so rightly: "Accept that values differ depending on your location. Appreciate it – different doesn't mean 'bad'. Just different."

The following traits can help to develop the process of acceptance: being tolerant, having an open mind as well as a great sense of humor (it can help tremendously when things go wrong or you end up in an embarrassing situation as a result of a lack of knowledge of the different social customs), being willing to communicate and to socialize, not being afraid to ask someone when you feel insecure and to approach others in order to build up a social network, showing a natural sense of curiosity and emotional/mental strength, as coming to live in a foreign country can of course be an emotionally demanding situation. If you know that you lack several of these qualities, you might want to rethink your decision for living in a different country.

The final stage of culture shock is the adaptation stage – you are integrated into the life of the host country, you accept its customs and the fact that some things are just different to what you are accustomed to. You might even actually discover that you are enjoying some of these differences. It is often laborious reaching this stage, but in the long run it is worth it. After you return to your home country you might even experience what is called a "reverse culture shock" – after feeling so comfortable with the culture in the host country, you have to get re-accustomed to the culture in your home country.

So, how does one reach the final stage of culture shock without going through an awfully hard time in between? I asked the expats in my questionnaire how they overcame culture shock and there were many helpful and valuable responses.

- *Take your time*
  It is normal to go through some difficulties at the beginning of your stay. As mentioned before, Germans are not easy to get to know and so you might take a while to make German friends and build up a multi-national network. Learning a language and getting accustomed to a new culture also takes

time, so don't expect everything to be perfect right from the beginning, start your stay with positive but reasonable expectations. As Bonnie Barski can say from her own experience: "Over time you gradually adapt – which is fine."

Sarah Happel, who has lived in several countries, has made a useful decision: "I have a personal rule to never make a judgment about my new residence abroad for the first year. It takes at least that long to get settled and get all the nagging issues out of the way, finding a house, registering, meeting the neighbors, settling in at a new job, developing a basis for the new language. How fair is it to judge the host country during this time? It's stressful no matter which country you move to and no matter how many times you do it. The second year is when you start to have some fun and feel more at home."

- *"Take German courses, naturally!" (Sarah Happel)*
  This should be self-evident but you would be surprised how many foreigners – often accompanying spouses – move to other countries and stay there for several years without ever making an attempt to learn the language. The perfect time to start learning German is before your departure, ideally as soon as you know about your move. You will find more about possibilities of learning German on pages 156 - 159.

  Once you have a basic knowledge of the language, it will take away some of the difficulties and anxieties you might have when buying food, talking to authorities or salespeople, meeting Germans and generally knowing what's going on. You will feel more secure, life will be easier and one of the biggest obstacles for your access to a new culture is cleared away.

- *Build up a social network*
  Ideally, you should begin with that before your departure as far as it is possible. The internet can be extremely helpful here. Visit expat forums and pages (for links see page 8) and find out whether there are expats in the area you are going to move to. Ask them about life in Germany and maybe you can even build up a friendship. If you have expat colleagues already in Germany or know German colleagues, ask them

questions and stay in touch. Join international clubs where you will meet many people in the same situation as you are. Robert Lederman did just that: "I had a large group of English speaking people that I could ask. Teachers, coworkers, friends, etc."

If there are many people you can ask whenever you feel unsure about something or who can advice you about where and how to find babysitters, shops or doctors, you will not feel so lost. Maureen Chase joined several organizations and found a babysitter and a *Tagesmutter* (child minder) to help her, which made her life a lot easier.

Although it is natural to move mainly within expat circles at the beginning, don't rule out the possibility of extending your social network to include Germans.

• *Be open-minded, tolerant and learn to accept differences*
This has already been mentioned, but cannot be emphasized enough. The more you are open to differences and even view your new multi-cultural lifestyle as an enrichment instead of a burden, the easier you will adapt. Chances are high that you will discover a few new customs that you get to like so much that you take them with you when you return home. Before I went to live in the USA, Thanksgiving didn't mean much to me as it isn't celebrated in Germany (we do have a similar holiday, called *Erntedankfest*, but apart from very rural communities, it is not acknowledged and not even an official holiday). I was very lucky that in my first year in the USA, American friends kindly invited me to their home for Thanksgiving. It was a fabulous evening, I saw this large warm-hearted family around their dinner table, chatting and laughing and exchanging the latest news and I got to eat all the typical dishes associated with Thanksgiving – turkey, sweet potatoes, cornbread, pumpkin pie, etc. I enjoyed myself a lot and was grateful to be able to spend the next Thanksgiving with the same family. When I returned to Germany, I wanted to keep up some of the Thanksgiving spirit and so had my own Thanksgiving meal, to which I invited my friends. Everybody had a great time and it has since become an annual event in my home, a little piece of America that I brought back to Germany.

- *Prepare and inform yourself*
  Chapter II informs you about the benefits of a thorough preparation and the sources where you can get information about Germany. You will not be able to anticipate every situation that you might experience in Germany, but several books and websites give you an idea of the main differences between the culture of Germany and that of your home country and thereby prepare you for unknown customs. Don't stop your information crusade once you arrive in Germany. You can always ask other expats and Germans about social rules or what to do when you are in a situation where you feel unsure. If you are like me, you might also benefit by asking about the reasons for certain customs, laws and regulations. If I know the reason behind something, it makes it easier for me to accept it. Of course, in Germany, like in every other country, there are several customs and laws the reason of which remain mysteries....

- *Don't indulge in Ethnocentrism*
  So, here you are in Germany. Your neighbor told you that your door mat is too dirty, it took you 20 minutes to buy some stamps because nobody at the post office understood you, the cashier at the supermarket got unfriendly because it took you too long to find the correct change and you live in a city where you don't know anybody and nobody seems to be interested in getting to know you. You don't know what to do with your time as you are not allowed to work and you are not mobile because your driver's license is not valid in Germany. It is not easy to like a country that puts so many obstacles in your way. You are close to writing your friend in your home country a long email, telling her how much better everything is regulated at home and how awful everybody and everything is in Germany. This is absolutely understandable and it will probably help you to vent a bit. However, don't let this become the dominating attitude during your stay. Instead of concentrating on what is so terrible, try to find out why a situation is so awful and see whether you can remedy it. There isn't much you can really do against annoying neighbors or the unfriendly supermarket cashier (except go to another supermarket),

but almost all of the other situations mentioned above will lose their negative impact once you are more familiar with the language, have met friends, know what the money looks like, have made a German driver's license and found a hobby or fulfilling volunteer work. Life will appear more friendly and you will realize that not everything is worse than in your home country.

- *Keep busy and also pamper yourself*
  The more time you have for brooding, the more time you have to feel miserable. Also, having nothing meaningful to do is a big strain in itself and can worsen culture shock. You can combine keeping busy with meeting new people. There are many ways of keeping busy – language courses, international clubs, volunteer work, playgroups (if you have children), taking up new hobbies or using the time to cultivate the hobbies you never had enough time for. Nevertheless, also take time to pamper yourself. As already frequently stated, moving to and living in a foreign country can be strenuous, so give yourself some time to relax. In the beginning you probably won't get as much done as you did at home, simply because daily matters will take more time for a while. Don't worry about it and allow yourself to rest whenever it is necessary. You can also combine pampering yourself and getting to know your surroundings by taking enjoyable little day trips or visit interesting sights in your new home town.

- *Expect culture shock but don't give into it*
  Prepare yourself for the fact that you will experience culture shock to some degree. Maybe it will just be a brief period of feeling uncomfortable and a bit anxious. Most of those who filled out the questionnaires reported no major difficulties with culture shock. Still, it will be noticeable, so don't let it catch you by surprise. However, as you see, culture shock can be overcome and there are many ways of getting out of it to acquire a wider horizon and collect treasurable new experiences. So if you notice the first signs of culture shock, don't give into it, work against it.

Chances are that once you reach the acceptance stage, many things won't bother you as much as they did at the beginning. However, there will of course always be certain aspects of the culture in the host country that you will never be able to or never WANT to accept. That's fine, after all there are probably also aspects of the culture in your own country that you don't approve of. As long as your attitude is predominately influenced by tolerance, curiosity and open-mindedness, it is only advisable to look at some things critically. One expat from England stated that while she grew accustomed to the direct and sometimes discourteous behavior of Germans, she never got used to the inflexibility.

In the next section, you will find an article from a woman who has been there and got through it all. She will give you some further valuable advice and will also amplify some of the points that were made in this section.

3. Culture Shock? What Culture Shock?

By Patricia Bartholomew

Nothing compares to the first time you move abroad: it is definitely one of the most exciting times in your life. It can also be one of the most terrifying. What do people find is the most difficult when moving abroad? Language? Culture? Shopping? Let's take them one by one. Undoubtedly, language plays a big role in assimilation, but look at Great Britain and the United States. Same language (at least some say so), but it is still a great shock for British citizens who move to the U.S. and vice versa. Same with Germans and Austrians, Portuguese and Brazilians, the list goes on. If not language then, is it culture? Some people think: if I could just master the culture then I won't have any more problems in my new country. It could be. Shopping? Personally I think when you can walk into a store without that cold rush of adrenalin that comes right before something goes terribly wrong—for example this time you will certainly ask for that cheese at the counter and the clerk will understand me (unlike the last five trips to the store) --then you have come a long way in assimilating.

Many people fool themselves into thinking: if I can just master this one thing then my life will be so much easier. My problems will be solved. The simple truth about culture shock is that there is no one single thing to master. If there were, moving abroad would be so much easier. What makes moving so hard is the million little everyday things that you never have think about at home: What was the word for cheese again? Can I say hello to people I don't know but pass on the sidewalk? Will they think I'm rude if not? If I do, will they think I'm a stalker? Can I ask people "How are you"? Or is it too personal? Which side of the sidewalk do I walk on? What is everyone saying around me? Which way do I look when I come to an intersection? All these things and more now you have to think about—and worse, you have to think about them all the time. There is no rest, even at home in your apartment simple things like throwing something away can become nerve wrecking when you know you are supposed to sort your garbage but are not sure how. To make matters worse, in most cases learning these new things requires unlearning old things. Your first reaction, while perfectly adapted for your home country, must now be rethought. You can no longer simply act. In fact you must think to control your first impulse and redirect your actions to the new environment. Totally infuriating, especially when nobody else around you seems to have these problems. These million tiny things, unlearning, relearning, all day, everyday will drive you nuts and quite frankly, send you straight into shock—culture shock. And the funny thing is you'll be so busy dealing with these million things that you won't notice the culture shock. You simply won't have the time to notice. Culture shock? What culture shock? I don't have time for that. I've got to figure out this public transportation system today. Although, one day about six months after your move you will be walking around and feel like a fog has lifted and you will know—hey that must have been culture shock. That is the secret face of culture shock. You won't know it until it's over.

Depending on how hard you get hit with it, culture shock can feel like mist, fog, a snowbank, or a mound of dirt covering you. There are some tips that can help you tunnel your way out of culture shock faster.

- Watch the locals. this may seem obvious, but it took me my third or fourth move before I realized the value of this. For example, if you are at the bus stop for the swimming pool, but have no idea which way to walk, look for the people in swimming suits and floats and follow them. Or if you are shopping and you have a shopping brimming with goodies and everyone in front of you has only 3 or 4 items, you may want to check you aren't in the express lane.
- Listen to the locals. If you are at a café, and the five people ahead of you order coffee. You certainly will have a good idea how to ask for your coffee when the waitress gets around to you. Also pay attention to the questions the waitress asks the other people and their answers. There is a good chance she will ask you the same.
- Study the language. Even though I said earlier that language was not the single most important thing to culture shock, it still remains an important part. I heartily recommend an intensive course first thing when you get to your new country. This will get you immersed as quickly as possible and you will avoid how to improperly say things that work, but will be very hard to unlearn later on. Intensive courses are not, however, practical for everyone given the time requirements. Try to study at least an hour a week though. The first thing you should learn is: *Ich kann nicht sehr gut Deutsch sprechen*. This means I can not speak German very well (and try not to say it too well or no one will believe you). Use this often. Frequently the speaker will resort to English or give up and walk away.
  o Get your teacher to role-play everyday situations with you. For example at the bread, meat, cheese counter. How to ask for a bag at check out when you've forgotten yours (*Eine Tüte, bitte*). Restaurant, Post Office, etc.
  o Do not waste your time learning the names of exotic animals, fairy tale terms or other things you won't use everyday. If you like, you can learn them later.
  o Carry a small pocket dictionary with you at first. This is great immediate feedback for words you encounter frequently but have no idea what they are. Also great for quick reference if you are trying to ask for

something and can't remember the German word. If your pronunciation fails, just point to the word in the dictionary. Chances are the person will say it out loud and you will have a good idea how to say it next time.

o   Use online translators. I once had an entire conversation with someone using one. Also good for newspaper text. They aren't exact, but at least it gets you in the vicinity of meaning.

- Bring measuring cups, etc from home. I made the mistake of bringing my cookbooks, but no cooking implements. I spent about a year trying to convert everything into metric before I wizened up and brought my cups and tablespoons back with me one vacation.
- Get involved. Find groups of people that like to do what you like to do. This gets you out in the local community, outside of work, and can give you a whole new perspective on the country. Even if you can't speak the language, you can roller blade, scuba dive, play tennis, paint together and do what you like without too great a need for communication.
- Get a library card (saves you tons on Amazon). The libraries in the bigger cities have a good selection of foreign language titles. You might have to bring a copy of your Anmeldung and a small bit a cash ~10 EUR.
- Find a group of people from your own country. When you've had enough of integration, treat yourself to a few hours speaking your home language and a tiny bit of complaining. Be careful though — it can be habit forming — and when used to exclusion of all else a guaranteed way not to enjoy your time abroad.

Despite everything you do, there will be frustrating days — days you just want to book the first flight home. Failing that, you may just want to spend the day under the covers. Many people from other cultures can find Germans blunt to the edge of rudeness and meanness. More than one time I have wanted to crawl under the covers because someone agreed with me when I said I had done something dumb. I guarantee you, although it may seem rude in your home culture, they are not trying to be rude and they are just as blunt with their fellow

Germans. You may have to take a deep breath and then feel free to let them know what you think too. (This is a definite incentive to learn German and can be very liberating — especially for those people from cultures where you don't ever say directly what you think.) There will also be days when you can't get the simplest thing done. And you know what? If you need to spend a Saturday in bed, do it. Give your brain a rest from the continual barrage of new information. A Saturday spent this way can go a long way to improving your mood. Be careful though, if you find you are spending every Saturday for two months in bed, it may just be time to get out and find out where those tennis courts are.

4. Peculiarities of German Culture

You are aware that the German culture is different from the one in your home country. Maybe you know Germany already from previous travels, maybe it will be the first time for you to set foot into the country that will be your new home. Undoubtedly you already have some ideas and expectations about Germans and German culture. In my questionnaires I asked whether the expats noticed any differences between their home culture and German culture (of course all of them did) and whether they could name anything they found typically German. The answers were manifold, depending on the respondents' home country and where she or he lived in Germany. Two things that were almost always stated were that Germans are very private and also that they are unfriendly (as has been mentioned before). These issues seemed to have made the strongest impression on expats and also featured as being the main cultural difference. Therefore they will be at the top of our little list of peculiarities of German culture. I will give you some background information and explanation about German peculiarities and I hope it will help to give you a first impression of what you will expect in Germany.

a. Unfriendly and private Germans?

"I think the main [problem] was how direct / discourteous Germans are."
"People were very unfriendly and unhelpful."

"[The] biggest difference is the non-openness and unfriendliness of the German people."
"People seemed at first not as friendly, especially in shops."

These are some of the statements made in the questionnaires when asked about the first impressions of Germany and cultural differences noted. In a similar survey among Germans about their experiences during their stays in other countries, they almost always pointed out how much friendlier people in these countries seemed to be compared to Germans. Therefore it clearly has to be said – Germans don't come over as the most friendly people on earth. However, it isn't as bad as it looks. Many expats pointed out in the questionnaires that – after a while – they discovered that Germans actually were not per se more or less friendly than other nations, it just took a while to find that out. The last quote I put in the list above was made by Alice Waldron from the UK. I think is sums it up best – at first, Germans do not seem friendly. So what is it that gives us this first unfavorable impression of unfriendliness?

In my opinion, the reason lies in the general reserved attitude Germans have. Just recently I talked to an American friend who had returned from a journey to Ireland. She had gone to a pub with some friends and after a while another person came up to their table and chatted and joked with the others. To my friend's surprise he said after a while: "Oh by the way, my name is Mike." He hadn't known any of the people at the table and yet they had chatted as if they were best friends. I myself was often aware that although I frequently had most animated conversations with total strangers in waiting lines, at bus stops etc. during my stay in the US, this would never happen to me in Germany (actually, by now it does happen occasionally – are we Germans changing?). It is just not part of German culture to be extremely open to strangers. Germans are not into small talk and they also highly value their own privacy. They usually wouldn't dream of starting to talk to someone they didn't know, as it could be seen as an invasion of the other person's privacy and in most cases it would end up in some meaningless dialogue, which simply wouldn't make much sense to Germans (after all, not many deep meaningful conversations have developed between total strangers in waiting lines). They would only talk to a complete stranger if there was a certain reason for addressing that person – asking for directions, inquiring whether it was the right waiting line or to get some other information. However – this of course is not valid for all Germans and some expats will make completely different experiences. Sarah Happel told me: "I have strangers talk to me almost every single day, at the grocery store, at the park, at the drugstore, on the U-Bahn. Maybe it's because I have kids and so many people come up and talk to my kids. But even alone, people – mostly elderly, but sometimes my own age too – start talking about something. – Do you know I've had older people open up their purses and give my son 50 cents to go buy something at the store? Or some chocolate or a bite of something sweet? This strikes me as very friendly and every single time we go to the bakery or meat market they give my son a free pretzel or a piece of Wurst."

So you see it cannot be said generally that all Germans are reserved. It also depends on where the expats comes from and what their own cultural background is with regard to approaching others and respecting privacy. Again, Sarah Happel – married to a Fin – offers some valuable insight: "Germans may seem cold to someone coming from Italy or France or even the USA, but people coming from Nordic countries find Germans very warm and talkative."

There is a custom of exchanging greetings in certain situations, but nobody would necessarily expect a conversation to follow the greeting. Maureen Chase noticed this custom of exchanging greetings and considered it a sign for what I just said – people are polite and reserved. She said: "I notice that people say 'Guten Tag' or a similar greeting when entering a doctor's office, and everyone else in that room responds the same! Funny. In the supposedly friendly US we don't do that. You just walk in and have a seat. When entering a store [in Germany], you always greet the person who works there, and they greet you. You say goodbye as well."

I would even go so far as to say that the lack of customer service many expats criticized has to do with the strong value for privacy (although there definitely is a lower standard of customer service in Germany than in many other countries). When I went shopping in the US, at first I found it charming how I was welcomed with a cheerful "Hi, how are you!" as soon as I stepped foot into a store and I found the questions as to whether I was looking for anything specific or whether the salesperson could be of any assistance very attentive. After a while, though, it got on my nerves a little. I prefer being left in peace when I browse in a shop and I think many Germans share this. They want a salesperson to be courteous but to stay in the background until the customer asks for assistance. The lack of customer service in Germany however is mainly commented upon by Americans who are used to excellent customer service in their home country. Expats from European countries don't really find German customer service any better or worse than that in their home countries.

So, don't be surprised if you will find people you encounter in daily life to be lacking a certain openness for small talk or the customer service you are used to. It is a combination of being reserved and of valuing their and your privacy. What might appear unfriendly to you is the manifestation of a long tradition of not wanting to be intrusive and of opening up only to people one knows well. Don't take it personally! In fact, as some expats told me, a good way of dealing with this reserved behavior is to realize and keep in mind that it is not meant personally. I had an experience in England once where I felt somewhat insulted by something that was not meant in a rude manner, but was just the customary way of exchanging greetings. I was still a teenager and visited my mother's English friends with my parents. My mother's friend greeted me with "How do you do?" and I, assuming that she inquired about my well-being, started to tell her that I was in fact doing fine and had had a lovely trip etc. etc. However, I didn't get far with my statement as she had already proceeded to the next guest to exchange greetings. I thought it was discourteous to ask me how I was and then not listen to the reply. Later I learned that the "How do you do" English people say to each other as a greeting is not an inquiry but just a form of greeting, like "Hallo" and you are meant to reply with "How do you do?" and nothing else, just as Americans expect you to reply to an "How are you?" with a "Fine. How are you?", even if you are not fine at all. If you are an American or an English person, you will not consider these greetings rude and of course they are not rude at all, but a person not used to them might think differently. It's the same with German reserved behaviour. It is not meant in an unfriendly way, it is just a customary manner.

You will notice that this German attitude can make it difficult to find German friends (but I advise you to try and make German friends while you are in Germany as it will be far more beneficial in overcoming culture shock and exploring your host country's culture than just socializing within expat circles). How are you supposed to meet Germans if they are so reserved? There is an extra chapter on that starting on page 135, so I will just say here that it will take persistence, but it is, of course, possible and, as Bonnie Barski says: "Once you know them, they're like people everywhere." Andrew Brocklehurst, who came from the UK, has reached a conclusion that I hope many of you will get to share during your stay in Germany: "Germans are friendly if you are."

b. Hierarchical and Formal Structures

When you are introduced to an American, he will usually immediately tell you to call him by his first name. This custom applies throughout all levels, it is absolutely normal for people to call their bosses or even the company's CEO by their first names. You won't experience that in Germany. Germans are formal, they won't ask others to call them by their first names unless they have become good friends (although among younger people, a first-name basis is reached far sooner, even in working surroundings and it is also a matter of company culture). Neighbours can live next to each other for decades and still address each other by *"Frau ..."* (= "Mrs. ...") and *"Herr ..."* (= "Mr. ..."). They would probably be surprised and even taken aback if their neighbour would suggest switching to first names.

As Germans generally reserve the first-name basis for people they know well and are friends with, it isn't easy for them to call someone by their first name if they don't like this person or if they don't know whether this person likes them. It happened to me once that a person I didn't like at all suggested that I call her by her first name. I felt extremely uncomfortable doing so because for me, like for many Germans, this is a sign of mutual liking. The formal way of addressing people demonstrates the desire for keeping a certain distance, thus complying with the German reserved behaviour and strong sense of privacy.

If Germans do decide to revert to the more familiar way of addressing each other, there is a special ritual for that (again, this ritual is not widespread among young people), called *"Brüderschaft trinken"* (drink the pledge of close friendship/brotherhood): both raise their glasses and announce their first names ("I'm ..."), even if the first names are already known to the other person. Afterwards, both drink from their glasses and hug each other or sometimes exchange cheek kisses. As you see, Germans even have a formality for becoming more informal.... However, you will most probably not encounter this ritual much, if at all; if Germans offer to move to a first-name basis they will just tell you "You can call me ...".

As mentioned before, it takes a while before Germans get to this stage and therefore it might be a good decision not to suggest to people you don't know well for them to call you by your first name unless you are absolutely sure they are comfortable with it. Even better – wait until they make you this offer. People who can get touchy about being called by their first names are your superiors at work, people older than you and also people who work for you.

First and last names are not the only distinction that is made in ways of addressing each other. Unlike English-speaking people who only have the "you" form, Germans have two words for this, the informal *"Du"* and the formal *"Sie"*, just like the French *"Tu"* and *"Vous"*. Going on a *"Du"*-basis is handled just as reluctantly as going on the first-name basis and usually both go together; if you call someone by their first name, you usually address them with *"Du"* whereas you use *"Sie"* for people you still address with *"Herr ..."* or *"Frau ..."*. There are some people who mix these forms of addressing others with their first name and still using the *"Sie"*; probably in order to keep some distance even when on a first-name basis.

Generally, you can assume that unless you are invited to do so, addressing someone with *"Du"* is considered extremely rude. The guidelines for when to use first names are just as applicable when it comes to using the *"Du"*.

You will probably encounter some people who have titles, like "Dr." or, if you are studying or working at university, "Prof.". Most Germans who have a title value it very highly and expect people to address them with this title. This tendency is especially strong in all academic environments.

Generally, with regard to offering a more familiar way of addressing each other, the general rules of politeness are applicable: usually, the older person makes the offer of using the *"Du"*, the one more superior in the work/university hierarchy or, in the case of both genders involved, the woman. – Most Germans are aware that other countries are less formal, and they will surely forgive you if you are not familiar with all the intricacies of how to address people. Still, it can never harm to be aware of those distinctions and to try to adhere to them.

c. The state will take care of it

"They (Germans) rely on the state to do everything so there is not much space for individual initiatives."

One of the main principles of Germany as a state is the principle of social justice and the welfare state. As the social security system based on this principle has been in effect since the 1880s, Germans have grown used to the state taking care of them. There is health insurance, pension insurance, accident insurance, long term disability insurance, unemployment insurance and several other insurances and provisions to make sure that Germans are well provided for in sickness, old age or unemployment. Most of these insurances are mandatory and a large portion of each pay check is spent on them.

It has become more and more obvious that this welfare system is not working any more. The reasons for this are manifold and would exceed the purpose of this book, but among them are the fact that there are more older people and less young people, which endangers the future of the pension system. Also, health care is getting very expensive and the statutory health insurances have been cutting back their services, which caused affluent young people to flee into the arms of the private health insurance, depriving the statutory health insurances of valuable paying members. Unemployment has been a serious problem for many years and the situation doesn't look promising for the German job market.

All these developments have caused the state to reduce its welfare benefits. It is already clear that people currently under 40 – 45 years of age will not get a sufficient old-age pension and long term disability insurance also had to undergo extreme cuts and is not applicable for the majority of the population in the future. For a people that has been used to the state taking care of their welfare for many generations, it is difficult to get used to the idea of having to provide for these things themselves. For the average person it is also a question of money, as although health insurance and pension insurance get less reliable, they are still mandatory for the majority of Germans and therefore substantial amounts have to be paid for them, leaving people without the financial means for additional private insurance.

If you come from a country where self-reliance has had a long tradition, you might be confused about the large amount of mandatory insurances (as a foreigner living in Germany only for a limited amount of time, you are exempt from certain insurances and can get reimbursements for others after you return to your home country) or about Germans complaining about the state leaving them alone with their worries. You will probably also notice that relying on the state has a great influence on the development of volunteer work or private charity associations. Volunteer work, so popular in the US, is hardly known in Germany and private initiatives for charitable causes such as fund raising, social events or charity balls are not very common (and of those that take place, many are initiated by international clubs). I noticed this when I helped with the fund raising for a Gala Ball the AWCT (American Women's Club of the Taunus) organized. This was when I first learned about fund raising, until then the concept of just asking companies or stores to donate money or items was absolutely foreign to me.

d. Separation of work and private life

"The Germans seem less interested in having social relationships with their work colleagues."
"Work colleagues did not arrange as many social activities as in England. And it takes longer for colleagues to get on a more 'personal level.'"

In Germany there is a saying: *"Dienst ist Dienst und Schnaps ist Schnaps"* basically meaning "Work is work and schnapps is schnapps". This illustrates how Germans generally separate their work life and their private life. Even if they get along well with their colleagues it doesn't necessarily mean that they socialize with them outside working hours as well. Again, this is something that is less applicable to younger people, but it is still something that many expats noted and commented on. There are two main reasons for this separation.

First, for many Germans the people you meet through work are just that – people in connection with work. In accord with the general reserved behavior of Germans, they don't see any reason to import work relationships into their after-work life. You won't find the after-work party or pub culture you see in the US or in the UK – at least not to the same extent. After work, people go home to their families or indulge in their hobbies, they don't usually want to hang out with their colleagues.

Secondly, compared to many other countries, especially the US, Germany is not a mobile society. Many people spend their whole life or most of it in the town or area they were born in and so by the time they start working they have already established a close circle of friends from school, their neighbourhood or university. Deeply rooted in this circle of friends they simply are not much interested in making friends in the work environment. This of course again depends on the age level and also the location. I live near Frankfurt and my friends here are from all over Germany, hardly anyone of them grew up in the Frankfurt area. It is much easier to make friends with colleagues in large cities, as the cities attract many young professionals from all areas and young people are generally more easy-going. Another important point to consider is the fact whether people already have families of their own or not. A colleague with a spouse and one or two children will probably spend a majority of his or her time with the family.

So don't take is personally if you feel that your colleagues are less interested in socializing. Chances are that this option has just not crossed their minds. Maybe if you suggest an after-work activity to your colleagues they will be pleasantly surprised. It can't harm to try, as long as you know that a declination of your suggestion is not meant in a rude way.

e. The positive and negative aspects of thorough organization and planning ahead

"My impressions of Germany? – Efficiency and great beer!"

If you want to move out of your German (rented) house or apartment, the minimum notice period usually is three months. At your workplace, usual notice periods are often between six weeks and three months to the end of the quarter, people having worked in companies for a long time or in very high positions can have notice periods of up to six months to the end of the quarter. In some companies you are required to let them know at the beginning of the year when you plan to take your vacation within that year. If you want to switch your health insurance, the notice period is three months.

These are just a few examples of how much Germans like to plan ahead. Chances are high that you will be stunned at these long notice periods. When I lived in Boston and had to return to Germany, I wanted to phone my landlord to let him know I was moving out. Having become culture-savvy enough to realize that a three-months notice was not necessary in the US, I phoned him two months ahead and told him about my moving out. He asked when I planned to move out and I said "July 31st". Absolutely surprised he replied: "It's the end of May now! What are you calling me now for?" When I told him about German notice periods, he had a good laugh.

Germans don't like surprises and they want to make sure they do everything possible to prevent unwanted outcomes, some examples are the long notice periods for any kind of change, a myriad of laws to regulate every possible case or even the system of the welfare state. Intercultural experts call this characteristic "uncertainty avoidance" and it is strongly developed in Germany. Like most cultural traits of nations this one probably has geographical and historical reasons. Germany, with its location in the middle of Europe (surrounded by many countries), was always in a vulnerable position due to the many borders it shared with these countries. Also, Germany itself was not one whole country until 1871, but rather a conglomerate of smaller and larger kingdoms, duchies, principalities etc. This created a situation that just called for all kinds of unpleasant surprises and in order to get along Germans had to develop a strong sense to plan ahead and to avoid any uncertainties as far as possible. Also, if you have read the history chapter in this book, you will have seen how often Germans lost everything through war, unrest of inflation. Therefore, their strong sense for "uncertainty avoidance" doesn't come as a surprise.

The thorough regulation and organization of life is something most expats notice quickly and look upon with mixed feelings. Whereas the efficiency resulting thereof is very welcome and appreciated, the lack of flexibility is often criticized. It's hard to make spontaneous decisions if you have to consider notice periods, obey regulations and similar aspects. If you find a lovely new apartment which is available right now but have a three-month-notice period for the old apartment, you might end up losing the new apartment or having to pay rents for two apartments for three months. If you apply for a fabulous new job in July, but won't be able to start before January due to your notice period, chances are high you won't get that job. However, things are not as bleak as they seem. Germans can be more flexible than expected. A landlord might let you out of the rental contract earlier if you provide him with a new tenant and most companies won't hold an employee against his will.

Depending on where you come from, it will be hard to get used to this uncertainty avoidance and to succumb to long-term planning and all kinds of regulations. Believe me, it's frustrating for some Germans as well. The best you can do is to enjoy the efficiency that comes with it and to practice your own uncertainty avoidance by ensuring you are informed of any notice periods applying to your situation and you know all the rules and laws regulating daily life (or know someone you can ask).

f. Employee-oriented Employment Law

"More vacation time, sick days, honeymoon days!"
"Working for a temporary agency I got full benefits!"

On the previous pages the long notice periods employees have here were already mentioned. Generally, German employment law is employee-oriented, trying to ensure that there is no chance of hire-and-fire mentality development. A German employee can't be fired unless there is due cause (however, this doesn't apply for all companies; currently companies with less than 10 employees are exempt from the regulation, it also doesn't apply to the first six months of a work relationship, which is called Probezeit, meaning probationary period). There are only three groups of due cause: a) company-related reasons (reduction of business etc.), b) person-related reasons (lack of necessary abilities) or c) behavior-related reasons (culpable violations of contract). Even if one of these reasons is given without doubt, there are further considerations and procedures to be adhered to. The notice period must still be acknowledged unless the situation makes it unbearable for the employer to continue the work relationship. Today, many people consider this strong employee protection law one of the main reasons for the high unemployment. They say companies are reluctant to hire people because it is not easy to fire them again if the work relationship doesn't work out well. A loosening of employment law is demanded regularly.

As you can see in the second quote above, even temps get full benefits, it is required by law. I was a temp in the US for a while and inquired about health insurance. I think they were surprised about this question as temps just didn't get health insurance from the temping agency. Here, a temp has the same full benefits as a regular employee – vacation days, notice periods, maximum work hours, insurances. Temps also have to be paid a salary if the temp agency doesn't have a job for them, which is why by now most temping agencies are more reluctant to give out employment contracts until they can ensure that they have sufficient temp jobs available.

To my knowledge, Germany has the highest amount of regular vacation days. Whereas the law stipulates a minimum of 24 vacation days per year, I have never worked for a company that granted less than 27 vacation days a year. There are also additional days, called Sonderurlaub, special vacation. They vary from company to company and apply to special events such as marriage, birth of a child, a move or the death of a close relative.

This just outlines the main benefits of German Employment law and might help you to understand the discussion currently raging in Germany about the strong employee rights hindering the creation of new employment. A more detailed overview about Employment law is given on pages 174 - 184 and might be of interest to you if you are working in Germany.

g.   Punctuality

Punctuality is extremely important in Germany. Showing up late is considered rude, unless you have a very good and reasonable excuse for your delay. When a German tells you to meet him at 4 pm, he means 4 pm sharp. You should definitely be there on time or, if that is not possible, you are expected to call and let the person waiting for you know why you are delayed and when you will be there. Germans notice delays, even little ones, and don't look upon them lightly. A major point of discussion here is the apparent delay of many trains of the Deutsche Bahn (the German railway company). It is considered to be a serious problem, even though most delays are just a matter of a few minutes. An acquaintance of mine from India once told me an interesting story about his journey to Germany. He took the train from one location to the other and on the way, the train stopped in Frankfurt. According to the timetable, the stop was to be two minutes. My Indian acquaintance, probably used to a more lenient approach to time, was sure that the stop would give him enough time to get out at the station, buy a snack and come back to the train. He was convinced that a 2-minute stop didn't literally mean he would only have two minutes time. So, he got out of the train and sauntered in the direction of the station hall. Fortunately, he stopped after walking a bit and looked back in order to memorize the number of his track. To his surprise he saw an employee of the Deutsche Bahn standing next to the train, looking up at the large station clock and then starting to give the signal for the train to leave after exactly two minutes had passed. Only by quickly jumping into the train did my acquaintance prevent being left behind in Frankfurt. To me it was a marvelous example of how exact Germans deal with time. 4 pm is 4 pm sharp and two minutes means two minutes.

h. „It's not even their business, is it?" – The habit of correcting others

"People, strangers, would 'correct' you if you break a rule = very new for me and very hard to get used to!"

A German habit I was never really aware of before it was brought to my attention by many of the expats who filled out my questionnaire: neighbors or total strangers pointing out to you that you did something wrong. When I thought about it, I also remembered German friends telling me about similar incidents. Neighbors of a friend of mine once rang her doorbell to tell her that her doormat wasn't 'sufficiently clean'. Another friend of mine once had a note under her windshield wiper telling her that she shouldn't park on the sidewalk in front of that house as it would 'damage the sidewalk'.

A French expat told me about being verbally attacked by a total stranger in a bakery because that person thought she spoiled her child too much, even though she was talking to the child in French and the person hadn't understood a word.

Yet another friend of mine had put up a net on her balcony so that her cats could go on the balcony without danger of falling off. It was a transparent net, hardly visible and yet neighbors complained that it spoiled the uniform front of the apartment building.

You will probably wonder why those people were complaining about these petty things that really were none of their business and I have to admit, I wonder as well. I assume that such behavior is grounded in the deep respect Germans have for law and order (remember the uncertainty avoidance). Most Germans basically follow laws – both the official and the social ones, they only cross the streets when the pedestrian light is green, they adhere to parking restrictions, they make sure that their house and garden look orderly and don't clash with the neighborhood houses, they expect that other people should also do what is 'right' and expected of them. If you are new to Germany and not sure about all the laws and regulations and if somebody tells you nicely when you do something wrong, you might even appreciate the information, but generally most people understandably don't appreciate strangers admonishing them. Surprisingly, this conduct is in contrast with the general reserved and private behavior of Germans, in this case probably the wish for order is stronger than the respect for the other's privacy. Also, people who inform you that you did something wrong consider their behavior to be polite and helpful, not intrusive.

i.   The liberal German

When you think about the stereotypes about Germans, "liberal" probably doesn't come to your mind straight away. Compared to other Europeans, Germans are not more liberal, but many expats from the US or Canada notice that the attitude about smoking, nudity or alcohol in Germany (and in Europe generally) is much more relaxed than in their home countries.

"It's a real shock what they show on TV here! (...) Germans (Europeans) don't find nudity to be dirty."

Once, I had a German *Cosmopolitan* with me when I traveled to the US as I had read it in the plane. On one page was an advert for some sort of body milk or soap and it showed a woman with a nude upper body. My American friend who browsed through the magazine was absolutely stunned and told me that nudity was not shown in American magazines or on TV. There is plenty of nudity in German magazines and on German TV, and I don't mean the sleazy adult magazines and shows. Respectable news magazines sometimes have pictures showing nudity, because basically nudity itself is not considered filthy. If you come from a country that handles the display of nudity more reserved, be prepared to be confronted with this aspect. Germany (especially the Eastern part) also has a longstanding tradition of FKK, meaning

Freikörperkultur (nudists). There are special beaches reserved for FKK (don't worry, you won't accidentally end up there, there are signs indicating FKK-areas, like *"FKK-Strand"*). Even if one is not a fan of FKK, nudity is seen as normal or even required in some setting: saunas and steam rooms usually forbid swimsuits.

"My brother-in-law took a flying leap when he saw a teenager buy a beer at the local petrol station."

In Germany teenagers are allowed to buy lighter alcohol like wine at the age of sixteen and alcohol in general at the age of eighteen. Alcohol is sold in grocery stores, supermarkets and petrol stations. There are no restrictions as I have sometimes seen them in the US, that one can only buy alcohol if one has a driver's license or ID from the same state. Of course, people are aware of the problems connected with teenagers drinking and there have been many campaigns to make teenagers aware of the danger of being drunk - even if they don't 'feel' drunk - and of the dangers arising from drinking. Another problem has arisen with so-called 'alcopops' – alcohol mixed with a high amount of sugar or fruity flavors. Teenagers drinking alcopops don't feel drunk and like the sweet taste. However, these alcopops contain enough alcohol to be dangerous, especially in combination with sugar. Teenagers getting dangerously drunk regularly during going out or on so called "flat rate" evenings in discos (all the alcohol you want for a fixed price) have been a big topic in the media for quite a while and tests have shown that even teenagers under the age of sixteen can easily buy alcohol.

j. Shop opening hours and holidays

"The shopping hours came as a big shock!"

After learning the basics about Germany, you probably won't be surprised to hear that there is a special law regulating shop opening hours, the *Ladenschlußgesetz*. For some decades, shops were open until 6.30 pm in the evenings from Monday – Friday and until 2 pm on Saturdays (with a 'long Saturday' once a month when shops were open until 4 pm). In 1989 the 'long Thursday' was introduced – against strongest opposition from the unions, salesclerks and shopkeepers, who feared longer hours without an adequate rise of business. On the long Thursdays shops were open until 8.30 pm. I remember the first long Thursday, there was something of a party atmosphere, with everyone rushing into the city center to enjoy the feeling of shopping after 6.30 pm on a weekday. Gradually, the shops were also allowed to open longer on Saturdays and at some point certain cities even kept their shops open on selective Sundays.

After several more years – and of course after endless discussions – shops were finally allowed to open until 8 pm on every weekday and in 2003 shops were also allowed to stay open until 8 pm on Saturdays. After that innovation came through, you could hear and see excited ads in the radio, TV or in newspapers where shops proudly announced "At our store you can shop on Saturdays until 8 pm!" The latest change came in 2007 – now shops can open until 10 pm on weekdays. This, however, is only applied in shopping areas of major cities, in malls and large supermarket chains. Interestingly, there was far less excitement about this than in 2003.

Smaller shops and shops in small towns still keep the tradition of closing at midday, either between 12 pm and 2 pm or between 1 pm and 3 pm. Many of them might also close between 6.30 and 8 pm. If you live in a smaller town you should make yourself familiar with the shopping hours there as they will generally be more restricted than in cities.

Sunday is still mainly off-limits for shopping and I don't think it will change much. A while ago, the German Supreme Court ruled against a bid for a twenty-four hour shopping rule that was brought in by a major German retailer. The only shops not required to stick to these shop opening limits are petrol stations, shops in railway stations and airports or shops that mainly sell tourist items. Still, more and more towns offer the occasional "verkaufsoffener Sonntag", where shops are open on a Sunday.

A friend of mine has lived in Germany for five years now and still hasn't adjusted to the fact that on Sundays, no shops are open, not even bakeries. She thinks the Sunday atmosphere in German cities and towns is dreary. An expat from Australia pointed out in the questionnaire that the national holidays are very much like Sundays and she is right. Sundays and national holidays are meant to be spent with the family. People sleep longer, have an extended breakfast together and indulge in leisure activities like walking, swimming, going on day trips or just relaxing. Town centers often look deserted and even in a big city like Frankfurt you will have a feeling of emptiness. I am always amazed at how different the Frankfurt city center can look on a weekday with masses of people bustling through the streets and on a Sunday or holiday with only a few pedestrians sauntering along. It is slightly different in the summer, of course, when ice cream parlors, beer gardens and cafés are open and people rush out to enjoy the weather, but a markedly quieter atmosphere is created by the simple fact that shops are not open on Sundays. Whereas many expats I know consider this annoying, I wouldn't even say it is a bad thing. Now that shopping hours are relaxed enough to offer working people a chance to get their shopping done without having to constantly rush, I think it's quite nice to have one day in the week when businesses are closed and people have time to really relax. When asked whether she had any advice about social life in Germany, one expat replied: "Plan for relaxing Sundays not doing much." It doesn't sound bad at all, does it?

k. Lunch and dinner – eating patterns

In many countries, the main meal is eaten in the evening whereas lunch often consists of a sandwich or any other kind of cold snack. In Germany it is just the other way round. Germans have their main meal at midday, the Mittagessen. It is usually a warm and filling meal, whereas dinner, the Abendessen, often consists of just a salad or some sandwiches.

Due to this eating pattern, the weekend lunches are often the only main meals the family can have together and in many families these weekend lunches are an important tradition.

1. Karneval, Spargelzeit, Weinprobe, Christmas – a German year

Germany can boast many special events/festivities throughout the year, some of which are influenced by public or religious holidays, others by culinary enjoyments. Several expats in their questionnaires mentioned *Karneval* (carnival, a mixture of Mardi Gras and Halloween) and *Spargelzeit* (asparagus time). Depending on where you live, you will experience further special events of the various kind throughout the year, like the *Weinprobe* (wine tasting) or in Hessen the time when the *Federweißer* (a very young wine, tasting more like a slightly alcoholic grape juice than an actual wine) is sold everywhere. Christmas is celebrated in a special way as well. Therefore, let me give you a little overview of the main highlights of the year.

The *Karneval* (*Fasching* in South Germany) season starts on November 11 at 11.11 am and lasts until Ash Wednesday (*Aschermittwoch*). The highlight is the Monday before Lent (*Rosenmontag*) when the traditional *Karneval* parades take place (in some towns, they can also take place on the days before). People dress up in costumes and celebrate with great exuberance, but there is a lot more to it than that. Actually, many people are involved in preparing and organizing *Karneval* throughout the year. In this country of clubs there are of course special *Karneval* clubs (*Karnevalsvereine*) that organize carnival parades and the traditional carnival parties. Political humor plays a big role in both events, many of the floats in the parade characterize images and figures of current affairs involved in main events of the previous year. The *Karneval* parties take place everywhere in large halls with an entertaining program – people play sketches and make jokes or hold speeches about the political situation, doing so in a humorous way but yet not afraid to criticize politics and politicians with a sharp tongue. These speeches are called *Büttenreden* and are held by amateurs. Another popular feature of these parties are the *Funkenmariechen*, young women dressed similar to cheerleaders, who dance. *Karneval* has a long and solid tradition in Germany whereby the tradition in each region differs considerably. The cities most famous for their *Karneval* are Köln (Cologne), Mainz and

Düsseldorf. They all have different salutations. Whereas in Köln one greets the *Karneval* parade or just expresses one's joy with '*Alaaf*', the appropriate salutation in Mainz and Düsseldorf is '*Helau*'.

Nowadays, almost every town has its parade and whereas the parades in the cities mentioned above can last several hours and are big events, attracting many people from near and far, the parades in smaller cities are correspondingly shorter. People in costumes are on the parade wagons or march in the parade and throw all kinds of goodies to the crowd lining the streets – traditionally they threw hard candy, but now they distribute all kinds of sweets, little bottles with alcohol, flowers etc. Children very much enjoy catching and collecting all the sweets during the parade.

May is the peak time for asparagus and that's when you'll discover signs everywhere, on the doors of grocery shops and restaurants announcing the *Spargelzeit*. Many restaurants offer special asparagus menus. Little booths appear along the streets where local farmers sell their homegrown asparagus and the magazines publish all kinds of asparagus recipes. I don't know of any other vegetables that receive such a cordial welcome as asparagus. If you like asparagus, try to buy it on a farm (some of them have little stores selling their own produce) or try out one of the booths along the streets. The homegrown asparagus tastes much better than the asparagus offered in supermarkets (the thicker they are, the juicier!).

During fall the little villages along the rivers Rhine (Rhein) and Moselle (Mosel) offer wine tasting sessions aplenty. The riversides of both rivers feature many vineyards and the German wines have not only become more and more popular in Germany but are praised worldwide. A journey along those rivers with their picturesque towns, vineyards and castles is always highly recommendable, but if you like wine, you should definitely go there during the wine tasting season. You will find tables on the boardwalks where cheerful people gather to try the latest Rheinwein or Moselwein. The atmosphere is special – informal and merry.

The year ends with the Christmas season. It has a tendency to start earlier every year, by now the first Christmas sweets can already be seen in numerous shops at the end of August and the best things are often sold out by the middle of December.

The 'core' Christmas season takes place between the first advent and Christmas day. This is the time when the famous German Christmas markets start and the streets and buildings in the towns and cities are decorated. Compared with other countries, the decorations here are not overdone, even though the latest trend seems to be influenced by the ample American Christmas decorations. Now, some homeowners cover their houses in a blanket of lights and place all kinds of large Christmas decorations on their lawn. These houses often become somewhat of a tourist attraction as that kind of lavish decoration is just not common here.

The *Adventskranz* (advent wreath) can be found in most private homes as well as public and office buildings and accompanies the Christmas season. It has four candles and traditionally, the first candle is lit on the first advent Sunday, a further candle on the second advent Sunday and so on, until all four candles are lit on the fourth advent Sunday. A special custom for the children (even though some adults enjoy this as well) is the *Adventskalender* (advent calendar). These come in all shapes and sizes. The most common version is a flat cardboard box the size of a small painting with a Christmas motive printed on the cover. There are 24 little doors on the front and as of December 1, every day one of the little doors is opened to reveal a piece of chocolate in the shape of a Christmas motive. Some calendars just have pictures behind the doors, others have fine pralines or special sweets; there is a wide selection. Many people also make the *Adventskalender* themselves by tying little cloth bags to a large piece of cloth or along a string and putting all kinds of different little presents into each bag.

December 6 brings another special event for children, as it is Nikolaus Day. Although the Nikolaus bears a slight resemblance to Santa Claus, their functions differ slightly. The main difference is that Nikolaus doesn't show up on Christmas Day (the *Christkind*, Baby Jesus, brings the presents on Christmas Eve) and he doesn't bring large presents, but rather little goodies like sweets, oranges, apples, nuts and maybe a small gift as well. He puts these presents in shoes that are placed outside the door, so on the evening of December 5, children put their shoes in front of their bedroom door and on the morning of December 6, they get up excitedly and rush to see what Nikolaus has put in their shoes.

As mentioned before, Christmas markets usually take place from the end to November to December 23. In smaller towns, however, it is more common for the Christmas market to only take place on the advent weekends or even only on one weekend. As the Christmas markets in smaller towns often have a more traditional and special atmosphere, I can highly recommend them, especially if they are located in lovely old or historic town centers that serve as a perfect background. Of course the Christmas markets in the cities also have a lot of merits. Generally, the Christmas market consists of several market stalls that offer all kind of artsy items, Christmas decorations, presents or food and drink. A special drink during Christmas time definitely is the *Glühwein*, mulled wine that now comes in a variety of flavors. Whereas red spiced wine used to be the only flavor offered, you can now try cherry wine, hot apple wine (in Hessen), berry wine or non-alcoholic Glühwein, which is generally hot cherry juice or something similar and tastes just as good. The smell of *Glühwein* belongs to every Christmas, just as much as the other Christmas specialties – roasted chestnuts, sugar coated almonds or waffles and crepes. Walking over a Christmas market is usually a pleasure for all senses.

m. Coffee and cake

What afternoon tea is to the British, coffee and cake (just called 'drinking coffee' – *Kaffeetrinken*) is to the Germans. If you get to know other Germans better, chances are that they will invite you to visit them for coffee. It is usually taken in the late afternoon, around 4 or 5 pm and as well as the coffee, there is cake (home made or bought) or pastries or cookies. It is far less formal than inviting someone over for dinner and can often be a first move towards friendship or just a nice way to keep up a friendly acquaintance, frequently among neighbors. It is also a longstanding tradition among many families at the weekends. After the weekend lunch, family members rest or go for a walk and then they return home for *Kaffeetrinken*. You can find several comfortable coffee shops in Germany, some of them old and traditional, some of them modern bakeries with a few tables in the room, offering coffee together with a selection of cakes. Especially in winter it can be cozy and pleasant to indulge in a hot coffee or chocolate accompanied by a delicious piece of cake. You will find a large selection of the latter - simple, but tasty cakes as well as elaborate creations with cream and marzipan.

This concludes our little glimpse of different aspects of German culture. Of course you will not meet the "typical German" who embodies all these cultural specialties (well....maybe you will, but not very often). Also, this list may not cover all aspects, maybe during your stay you will discover something else you consider typically German. If so, you are welcome to mail me at hwolf@wolfintercultural.com (or even ask for a whole questionnaire to fill out and share your experiences and opinions about your life in Germany) and let me know what should also be added to the list.

V. Bureaucracy and Laws

1. First impressions and tips

"Difficult, time consuming and confusing."

Bureaucracy is never something people enjoy dealing with, no matter in which country. It is something unavoidable and a move into another country makes it a further necessity to deal with authorities and laws. Naturally, foreigners have different experiences with authorities than natives do, as foreigners have to get work and residence permits, inquire about the regulations to bring pets into the host country and deal with other things a native never comes in touch with. Therefore it is no surprise that most foreigners find the bureaucracy in their host country more complicated and disagreeable than bureaucracy in their home country. In the host country they have to take care of many more issues and also have to face the difficulty of not being familiar with the host country's laws and/or the language.

I was therefore pleasantly surprised to learn from the questionnaires that people had quite a well-balanced impression of German bureaucracy, as about 50 % reported that they had good or neutral experience with German authorities. Still, the experience of the other half was considered negative. An important factor here was whether the expats had someone to help them with their bureaucratic matters, like a university or a relocation agency.

From the comments made in the questionnaires, the worst impression people apparently were left with was after dealing with the *Ausländerämter* (foreigners' office, the place where foreigners apply for their residence permit). Government officials were often described as very bureaucratic and "unable to admit they might have made a mistake". Again, this is something that is often said about government officials in other countries as well, and in my experience with German bureaucracy (in my previous job, one of my tasks was to obtain work and residence permits for the company's expats), I met three kinds of government officials – those who were very much as described above, those who generally just did their job and didn't care and those who were friendly, helpful and competent. The latter was actually the largest group. One example was the employee of an Ausländeramt. He had sent our Korean expat a letter informing him of his appointment and explaining what papers to bring. Then, not sure whether our expat would understand the – German – letter, he phoned me and asked me to inform the expat as well. I thought that was very considerate. An American friend of mine keeps being pleasantly surprised about the helpfulness and friendliness of people at the authorities she has to deal with.

Overall, I can say that even though the bureaucratic system in Germany may seem confusing, inflexible and inefficient, it works quite well and even smoother than in some other countries. Whenever you get frustrated, just remember that much of the confusion arises from not being familiar with the applicable rules, regulations and procedures as well as having language difficulties. It is not as bad as it seems at first glance.

It is important to make time and have patience when dealing with authorities, not just with the German ones, as Bonnie Barski states: "Sometimes I had to wait in long lines at the American Consulate or when getting my car registered at the TÜV. But I guess that's to be expected."

Maureen Chase made the discovery that at some offices "there was a special line for people with children. We had my son with me so we were taken care of right away."

The most important advice and one given by almost every expat is: know your German, at least some basic words or bring a dictionary or a friend or colleague who speaks German. Not all government officials speak a second language and some bureaucratic terms are hard to translate anyway.

Other advice given in the questionnaires was:
- "Grit your teeth and get through it. There is no point complaining, demanding special treatment etc. (...) There is no reason behind many of the regulations but they are the law of that country and as such must be respected."
- "Be polite and always have official ID and lots of papers with you." (I would add that when in doubt – bring all the official papers you have.)

- "Be patient. Making a fuss does not help you get things sorted faster."
- "Never ever assume anything!!! Always ask! It took me five years to figure everything out."
- "Read a book about what you need to comply with. If you do need to go to any sort of *Amt*, get there early in the morning and bring a good book! Also make sure you go to the right department and have the right forms filled out, otherwise you'll have to queue up all over again."

By the way, your embassy or consulate is the right address for many bureaucratic matters (i.e. registering the birth of a child, obtaining documents). Embassy websites or hotlines can give you an overview of their services.

2. Immigration and Work Permit Laws

Germany's immigration and work permit laws are very complicated as they regulate all kinds of different cases. Here, I will just give you a short overview of the law that will most probably apply to your case – coming to Germany to work, to study or as an accompanying spouse. Please be aware that this is not a complete guide to German immigration law and that it is always advisable to get the most recent information and the one applicable to your special case. The information given here reflects the status of January 2015.

a. Entering Germany

Whether you need a visa to enter Germany or not depends on your nationality. There are three main categories:

EU Citizens

Citizens of EU-countries can enter Germany without a visa and they can stay here for 90 days without a residence certificate. Afterwards, a residence certificate is needed, requiring an Anmeldung (registration) with the local authorities (also see page 104).

Citizens of countries listed in the "*Visum-Positivliste*"

The so-called Visum-Positivliste lists all countries of which citizens do not need a visa to enter Germany (unless they come to Germany in order to work or study, see next paragraph). Currently, apart from the EU-countries, the following countries are included: Albania, Andorra, Antigua & Barbuda, Argentina, Australia, Barbados, Brazil, Brunei, Canada, Chile, Costa Rica, El Salvador, Guatemala, Honduras, Hong Kong, Iceland, Israel, Japan, South Korea, Macao, Malaysia, Mauritius, Mexico, Moldova, New Zealand, Nicaragua, Panama, Paraguay, San Marino, Seychelles, Switzerland, Singapore, St. Kitts & Nevis, Taiwan, Uruguay, Vatican, Venezuela, United States of America.

In some cases, the visa regulations depend on the kind of passport (biometric, with a personal ID number), so it's best to check in advance. You can always find the most updated version of this list on the following website: www.auswaertiges-amt.de. The site is available in English as well. Under the "Entry & Residence" menu all relevant visa information is published. It is recommended to check this website for updates and for certain restrictions.

If you are a citizen of one of these countries, you don't need a visa to enter Germany, but you can only stay in the country for 90 days in a time period of 180 days (it doesn't have to be 90 days at once. Any 90 days within 180 days count!) and you are not entitled to work. If you come to Germany in order to work or study, you will need a visa unless you are from one of the following countries: Australia, Canada, Israel, Japan, New Zealand, South Korea, United States.

If you intend to stay longer and work in Germany, you will need a work permit and a residence permit. If you come to Germany because you already have a job here, you can enter the country a certain period before you start work and without possessing a residence permit, as long as you get both within 90 days and do not start work before you have the work permit. However, it is generally strongly advisable to start the application process for both permits as early as possible so that you can receive them as soon as you enter Germany.

Citizens of other countries

All citizens of countries that are neither members of the EU nor listed in the Visums-Positivliste need a visa to enter Germany. It is highly advisable to adhere to the visa regulations, because if you enter Germany without a visa or with a tourist visa, you will not get a work permit. So if you come to live in Germany, you should make sure that the whole visa process is handled thoroughly and that you are sure everything is handled according to immigration law. A German company giving you/your spouse a job here or the German university where you want to study will usually take care of these matters, but you will have to go to the German Consulate in your country to apply for a visa.

A list of German Embassies and Consulates can be found here: www.auswaertiges-amt.de under "About Us" – "German Missions Abroad".

b. Living and working in Germany

Here again, the country you are from determines what kind of permits you need. All foreigners living in Germany or staying here for longer than three months need a residence permit. EU citizens are entitled to this residence permit (called residence certificate), as it is a certificate of the free movement granted to EU citizens within the EU. In all other cases it is at the discretion – within the law – of the German authorities to decide whether a residence permit (and work permit) is granted (for example if you don't have a job and no other means of financial support, you won't get a residence permit).

EU citizens

As stated in the previous paragraph, EU citizens are entitled to a residence certificate (*Freizügigkeitsbescheinigung*) as long as they can prove that they have a job or means of support. The residence certificate for EU-nationals is a separate document.

EU citizens do not need a work permit to work in Germany, the residence certificate also allows them the right to work, as this is encompassed in the free movement right.

Non EU citizens

If you are not an EU citizen, you will need both a residence permit and a work permit if you intend to live in Germany. (There are certain exceptions to the requirement of the work permit, but they usually don't apply to expats as they are mainly connected to unlimited or special residence permits.)

You will not get the residence permit unless you have already registered with the authorities (you will have to take your *Anmeldebestätigung* – see page 104 – to the *Ausländeramt* to get your residence permit). There are several kinds of residence permits, however, for people who come to work in Germany or as an accompanying spouse, the *Aufenthaltserlaubnis* will usually be the one that's applicable. The *Aufenthaltserlaubnis* is limited, but after a longer residence in Germany, there is the possibility of receiving an unlimited *Aufenthaltserlaubnis*. Still, this will generally not be the case for expats who just come to stay in Germany for a limited number of years.

Students require a different kind of residence permit, it is called *Aufenthaltsbewilligung* and is more restricted than the *Aufenthaltserlaubnis* as it is only issued for a definite purpose (like university studies) and for a limited time. There is no chance of getting an unlimited *Aufenthaltsbewilligung*. Also, once the purpose of the *Aufenthaltsbewilligung* is served (in a student's case: graduation), the residence permit expires automatically.

There are different kinds of work permits. They can be limited in time (this is the usual case) and also to one employer or one location. If you get a job for a company in Berlin, for example, your work permit is only valid for that special company and only for Berlin, so if you decide to change jobs, the work permit has to be changed accordingly. Some work permits just have one of the limitations mentioned above and some are for all employers and for all of Germany. You should look at your work permit carefully in order to avoid any unpleasant surprises. Also, once you have your work permit, make sure it doesn't expire before your work period ends, because you are not allowed to work any longer until the work permit is extended. Usually, I would advise starting the application process for an extension about four to six weeks before your current work permit expires.

As of August 1, 2012, getting a work permit has become easier for people who have a German university degree or an academic degree that is acknowledged in Germany (see www.anabin.de for acknowledgement information) and have a job offer in Germany where they earn at least 47.600 € a year (37.128 € a year for qualified professionals in the fields of mathematics, IT, natural science or engineering, as well as doctors). They can get a Blaue Karte (Blue Card) which is applied for at the Ausländeramt after entering Germany.

Limitations also apply to your residence permit. Depending on the dates your permits were issued, your residence permit could expire at a different date than your work permit. Strictly speaking, once your residence permit expires you are not allowed to stay in Germany. Therefore, here as well, carefully check the expiration date and don't forget to start the application process on time. If you have a reliable employer and/or a good relocation service, they will keep track of expirations themselves and contact you when it is time to apply for an extension, but you shouldn't rely on this completely.

Legally, you are required to always carry your work permit with you (at least whenever you work). Your residence permit and work permit are stamped into your passport, which you should always carry with you anyway. (If your regular passport expires, the residence and work permit has to be transferred to the new passport.) Having all necessary documents with you can make things so much easier if any government official ever asks for verification that you are allowed to live and work in Germany.

3. Special German Laws

"Complicated at first but liveable with."
"I get along ok but it is not easy to get information about them."
"When in doubt, ask neighbors, colleagues or friends about details."
"I did and don't always obey them correctly as they can be complicated, but I try."

Every country has certain laws that are strange to foreigners. Of course you can get fined for breaking a law even if you aren't aware of it and in order to avoid getting into such a situation, it would be advisable to familiarize yourself with some of the regulations that are 'typically German'.

a. *An-* and *Abmeldung* (Registration and De-registration)

You will encounter several official procedures revolving around your move to Germany, some of which I already mentioned in the section about German Immigration Law. One of the first things you need to do after you arrive is to register at the local municipal authorities (*Ordnungsamt, Einwohnermeldeamt, Bürgerbüro* or *Rathaus,* depending on the town you live in). Every person living in Germany, Germans and non-Germans alike, must always be registered with their local authority. Many cities and towns in Germany already have their own websites (generally the name of the city with the ending .de) that inform you of where to go and of the opening hours. You can also call the Rathaus or the municipality (*Stadtverwaltung*) to find out where you have to register. You register by informing the authorities that you have moved to their town and notify them of your new address (take your rental contract or other documentation of your new address with you, just in case). Then they will give you a confirmation of your registration which is called *Anmeldebestätigung*, which basically just confirms your address in Germany. Without this *Anmeldebestätigung* you will not be able to receive your residence permit!

You will also receive your tax identification number (*Steuer-Identifikationsnummer*) which – if you receive payments from a German company – has to be given to your employer's payroll department. At the end of each year, you will receive a paper from the payroll department that lists your German income as well as all taxes or social security deductions for that year. You need this confirmation for your tax return.

When you leave Germany, you have to go to the local authorities to notify them that you intend moving away and that your current address will no longer be valid (this is called *Abmeldung*). If you move within Germany, the *Abmeldung* is no longer necessary, the *Anmeldung* however still is!

Basically, it is not a major procedure and as several cities have now introduced the so-called *Bürgerbüros* (citizen's offices), which are usually efficient and quick, waiting times are often not that long either. Still, when you first arrive in Germany, it is of course confusing. If you don't have the chance to use a relocation service to handle this for you, you might want to ask a friend or maybe someone from an international club to come with you the first time. Don't forget that this procedure needs to be done every time you move within Germany. Otherwise you will get fined, as Rod Dixon, an expat from Zambia, experienced: "Make sure you know all of the areas you need to be registered. I was fined €20 for not notifying the authorities I had moved."

b. Ruhezeit (Quiet Period)

There are some "quiet periods" in Germany, which means that no excessive noise is allowed during certain hours of the day, this includes using a drill or an electric lawn mower, playing very loud music or doing any construction work. The quiet periods are between 10 pm and 7 am on weekdays (this includes Saturdays) and between 1 pm and 3 pm (less strict than the night quiet period). Sunday in general is a quiet period! Therefore, you will see no construction work going on Sundays (unless the workers have a special permit).

If you have a party that's too loud during the quiet period, people can (and sometimes will) call the police to report a disturbance of the peace. Sometimes neighbors will inform you if they plan a party that might be quite noisy even after the official quiet period will have started, so that you can be prepared and won't complain. If you live in an apartment complex, you will probably receive the house rules (in German) in writing, they will also include details about the quiet period. There have been innumerable court decisions about what may and what may not be done in the quiet period. Whereas the running of a washing machine (but only one that doesn't exceed certain noise levels) might have to be tolerated in an apartment building on Sundays, the lawn mower will not be accepted on that day.

I quite enjoy the quiet period and don't find it difficult to adhere to it. It also depends on your neighborhood how strictly it is followed, so as always, it is advisable to watch and learn. Maureen Chase has even seen the positive side to it and says: "The quiet period is okay with me. When we were moving in it was hard to suppress my need to hammer and make noise on Sundays, because I wanted to get set up quickly, but I respected it. In the end, I find we have more family time on Sundays because more stores are closed and we can't make noise at home, we have to be quiet. I like it."

c. **Garbage separation**

"I'm really surprised that you don't find tons or garbage dumped on the side of the road. It's a major pain to get rid of anything here."

"Garbage disposal seems to be very user unfriendly. Recycled cans are only collected once a month and for a non-German the explanation of collection days and colors is confusing to start with."

Getting rid of garbage can indeed become complicated. Garbage is separated and sometimes it is confusing to figure out where which piece of garbage belongs. When asked about difficulties with special German regulations, almost all expats in the questionnaires pointed out that while they were very willing to adhere to the environmentally friendly German garbage separation rules, they sometimes were just too confused or uninformed. While cities hand out calendars illustrating the dates (usually with a color scheme) when garbage will be picked up, these calendars as well as any accompanying information are usually in German. As the rules are very detailed, even Germans can be unsure where to put their garbage. My parents live in an area where the garbage separation system is incredibly strict and complicated (they even have to disassemble yoghurt containers and put the different materials in three trash cans!). I hardly dare to throw anything away while I'm there because I never know which garbage belongs where.

You are expected to separate your garbage correctly and the garbage men may refuse to empty a garbage can that does not contain the designated trash. Therefore I want to give you a quick overview of the garbage separation system even though there are regional differences, so it is best to inform yourself about any such distinctions.

If you don't live in an apartment building (where garbage collection is organized for the whole building) you have to sign up for garbage collection (sometimes this can only be done by the proprietor of the house, so if you rent accommodation you won't usually have to worry about this.). When you go and register with the local authorities you can ask them where you get the forms for the garbage collection as this is handled by the cities. If the city you move to has a website you can check there where you have to go. Some cities also offer the downloading of the necessary forms.

Due to the mandatory garbage separation (explained below) you will get two garbage cans - one for *Verpackungsmüll* (non-paper packaging like yoghurt cartons, milk containers or tins) and one for surplus garbage (not paper or glass). In some cities you may also get a green garbage can for *Biomüll* which is compost. The garbage collection fees you have to pay depend on the size of the garbage can (which you can choose unless you live in an apartment building) and the frequency of collection (each week, every two weeks or every four weeks). As mentioned before, you will be handed a calendar that notes the dates for the trash collection, this calendar will then be mailed to you yearly.

Generally there is:
- "regular" garbage
- *Verpackungsmüll* = packaging (has to be clean)
- compost and
- items that are recycled such as paper and glass.

You will find special containers in your area for paper and glass (some apartment buildings even have their own paper container). Glass is divided into clear, green and brown glass. Be aware that it is forbidden to put glass into the containers during the quiet period and on Sundays and public holidays. Please note, though, that there is a deposit on certain bottles. I will supply more information about the deposit system later.

Everything that is neither glass nor paper nor *Verpackungsmüll* goes in the regular garbage can (unless you have a compost can or a compost corner in your garden). This does not apply to (electric) appliances or possibly toxic garbage (e.g. paint). The calendar for garbage disposal usually tells you how to dispose of those items, otherwise you can also contact the garbage collection company.

Large items like pieces of furniture, mattresses etc. do not go into the garbage cans, they are bulk rubbish (*Sperrmüll*). You have to let the garbage collection company know that you have bulk furniture and in what quantity, then they tell you when they can pick it up. You will be charged for this service and depending on the condition of the items you might want to inquire if a charity agency might have use for them, as they sometimes pick up such items for free.

Old clothes and shoes are also frequently donated. You will find special containers for them in certain areas, but there are also regular collections (*Kleidersammlung*) which are usually announced by a leaflet in your mailbox.

On most bottles and cans there is a deposit (*Pfand*), so you should be careful not to throw them away as you will get your deposit back after you return them to the store. Most stores now have convenient machines where you get rid of the bottle or can and you get a receipt that the cashier deducts from your purchases. Literally all non-alcoholic drinks now come in returnable bottles and cans. They are marked with the word "*Pfandflasche*", "*Pfand*" or "*Mehrweg*".

Bonnie Barski has some good advice as to how dealing with the deposit system could be more convenient: "When the deposit on bottles came, I began to have our drinks delivered in cases (...). You only pay the deposit once, and you get it back later. It's a convenient way to buy drinks. That way you don't have to buy heavy bottles in the grocery store."

There are also special drinks cash-and-carry stores (called: *Getränkemarkt*) where you can park right in front of the door and get a convenient cart for transporting several cases.

d. Buying, driving and maintaining a car

i) Driver's license
About two-thirds of the expats who filled out the questionnaires reported that their driver's license wasn't sufficient for driving in Germany. Most of them were annoyed by this, Sarah Happel mentioned that even though she has been driving for fifteen years in the US, she had to retake the

German driver's license from scratch. Another expat summed it up well when she asked whether her driver's license was sufficient to drive in Germany: "For skills, yes. By German law, no." Maureen Chase, whose driver's license also isn't considered sufficient by German law, said: "I have to take the test, drive and written and as a result, I am not inclined to get the license."

The German law about driver's license is very specific, depending a lot on which country you come from (if you are from the US or Canada, it even depends on which state you are from!). This may seem arbitrary, but there is a reason for this. Several years ago, the German government wrote to all countries and states, offering them to merely exchange drivers' licenses for nationals from those countries for German drivers' licenses. In return they asked for the same rule to be applied to German citizens in the same situation. Some states and countries replied in the affirmative and those are the ones that are listed below under the option of merely needing to exchange your license. Those who didn't reply or replied in the negative were not included into this agreement.

At the beginning of your stay in Germany, you can drive with your own driver's license and if you have a EU-country driver's license (or a driver's license from Liechtenstein or Iceland), it will be valid for your whole stay. If your driver's license if from a non-EU country you will have to get a German driver's license, unless you are only staying in Germany for a year, because after the initial six months you can obtain a six-month extension for your own license. However this extension can only be obtained once, so if you know you are going to stay in Germany for more than a year, it is advisable to get the German driver's license.

Sarah Happel advises not to wait with this too long and recounts her own experiences: "I got an international driver's license before I came to Germany; they told me at the office n the US it would be good for one year. When I got to Germany, I was told it would be good for only six months and then the Driving School told me that no policeman would recognize my international driver's license because anyone could have forged it, it wasn't official enough etc. So what's my point? Look into it right away, don't wait until the end of that first year of even six months to change your license because if you are from one of the countries/states where you have to redo your written and driving test, it can take a couple of months to get all of your documents in order, buy the texts, study, take driving lessons and then take the test. If you don't pass the test, you have to wait some weeks and then try again. (...) The US embassy web site has a very good outline of what you have to do and what the estimated cost would be. I am from one of the 25 [US] states that had to take a written and driving test and in the end it cost me about 600 Euros and two months to finally have my German license in my hand. And I did it as fast as I could. – You need a lot of documents here in Germany, eye exam, doctor's statement that you are in good health, CPR and first aid certificate (it doesn't have to be current, only you have to prove that once in your life you took it). So be prepared to do a lot of running around for these records."

You should note that even if your driver's license is fully recognized by German law, there could be difficulties, as Alice Waldron from the UK experienced: "I had problems with my insurance as it [the UK driver's license] was not recognized at first."

Even if your driver's license is valid in Germany, you might be required to have a translation of the license with you. This is the case if you are not from a EU-country or any of the following countries: Andorra, HongKong, Monaco, New Zealand, San Marino, Switzerland, Senegal, Hungary or Cyprus. As there might be more requirements, it is best to check with the authorities whether a translation is necessary. Translations can be made by internationally validated automobile associations, the authorities, translators or German consulates.

Depending on where your own license was issued, you
- can merely exchange it (Andorra, Guernsey, Isle of Man, Israel, Japan, Jersey, Namibia (some restrictions apply), New Zealand, San Marino, South Korea, Switzerland, Singapore, South Africa, USA [Alabama, Arizona, Arkansas, Colorado, Delaware, Idaho, Illinois, Iowa, Kansas, Kentucky, Louisiana, Maryland, Massachusetts, Michigan, New Mexico, Ohio, Oklahoma, Pennsylvania, South Carolina, South

Dakota, Texas, Utah, Virginia, Washington, West Virginia, Wisconsin, Wyoming], Canada [Alberta, British Columbia, Manitoba, New Brunswick, Newfoundland, Northwest Territories, Nova Scotia, Ontario, Prince Edward Island, Quebec, Saskatchewan, Yukon], Puerto Rico)

- have to take a written test (USA: Connecticut, D.C., Florida, Indiana (in some cases only), Minnesota, Mississippi, Missouri, Nebraska, North Carolina, Oregon, Tennessee)
- have to take a practical test: Taiwan (some restrictions apply)
- have to take a written and a practical/driving test (for countries not mentioned above)

The tests are taken at driving schools (*Fahrschule*) and you should ask whether they have special arrangements for experienced drivers, so that you won't have to go through the whole long and very expensive driving course. Robert Lederman advises getting an English copy of the Driver's hand book to prepare for the lessons. Some driving schools also give the lectures in English.

Once you have your German driver's license, there is yet another point to consider, as Sarah Happel points out: "Be prepared to fight to keep your homeland driving license. The authorities wanted me to hand over my Minnesota driver's license before they would give me my German license and I refused because in America your driving license is your most important form of ID, and I would have trouble not only driving there on each visit, but writing a check or getting into a bar or using a credit card. In the end I found someone sympathetic to my cause, who had spent some time in the US, so they let me keep it."

If you come to Germany as a company expat, the German company could issue you a confirmation that you will still do substantial driving in your home country and therefore need to keep your home country's driver's license.

The good thing about the German driver's license is that it does not expire, so once you have it, you can only lose it through major or frequent traffic offenses.

ii)   Been there, done that, got the license

One of the expatriates I worked with sent me this delightful
account of how his wife's experiences with the German license
procedures and test and allowed me to use it for this book.

Anything that involves officialdom is a big deal in Germany.
But the driving license is a 'really' big deal because once you
get it, then you have it for life. So the German authorities want
to make sure that you are fully qualified before rolling the dice.
   [My wife's license] is from Connecticut. This means that she
has six months to get her act together and obtain a German
license. Now you would assume that if the Germans let the
Brits drive without restriction then they would do the same for
Americans. After all, Americans traditionally drive on the same
side of the road as the Germans.... whereas the Brits.... Ah,
but no. [My wife] must take the 'Written Test'. And of course,
the written test in Germany is a very serious affair. Here, there
is order and precision. So, [my wife] began by ordering her
instruction book in English. This cost €100. Yes, €100. For a
driving test handbook. You could get Goethe's complete works
for less. She then had to get her eyes tested; presumably so
that they could verify that she can actually read the books. And
only then could she register herself as an applicant for
licensing consideration. From this point, it takes them a
further three weeks to recognize that she has registered, at
which point, she is eligible to apply to take the test. I am not
making this up. But it gets better because she actually has to
study. It's not just a question of her recognizing a few road
signs (which is the trickiest part of the Connecticut test) or
calculating braking distances (a tricky part of the UK test). No.
The word "examination" would be a better description than
"test". Each question has three or four answers and you must
decide which answer is right (it can be one, two, three or all of
them). Three wrong and you fail. Most people fail at least once.
   33% of the test involves situational photographs and a
question asking what you need to do. For example, let's pretend
you are looking at a picture of a road, and on it are a few cars
and an overhanging tree. The tree is large, but otherwise
ordinary. It's leafy and sticks out a bit over the road.

Connecticut has millions of them. But we are not in Connecticut, so let's take a closer look at the German test:

Select the correct answers to the following question: "You are driving and see the picture before you. What do you do?:
1. Brake because the tree is a hazard (Observation: this is easy because you always pick 'brake' - even if no rational driver would ever actually do it)
2. Signal or Indicate (Observation: tricky, because they don't specify signaling right, left or both at once. So this one must be a false answer because Germans are never this imprecise. Or are they?)
3. Ignore the tree because the overhang is greater than 4.357 meters above the road at its lowest point, ignoring wind movement and assuming that this is not the third Friday in Lent when the required minimum overhang is 4.359 meters in Hessen. (Observation: Definitely pick this one)"
So, how did you do?

[After road sign recognition] the remainder of it asks questions like "What is the minimum distance you may park from a pedestrian crossing?" with the optional answers being 2.167 meters, 2.168 meters or 2.169 meters.

But I do sympathize with [my wife] . Really, I do. In fact I even read her instruction manual, just for a giggle.

iii) Buying a car
If you have a sufficient driver's license or passed your German test, you will probably think about getting a car. The expats who bought a car in Germany reported that it wasn't difficult. The bureaucratic process that followed the purchase posed more problems than the actual finding and buying.
Whether you want to buy a new or a used car, the methods for finding it are usually the same. The main sources are newspapers ads and large car dealers. The internet is also catching up on becoming a valuable source for car information. Robert Lederman who has bought / leased three cars so far in Germany, considers his experiences "over all pretty good." He tried several different ways of acquiring a car: "Leased our first

vehicle. That way if we went back we could simply give it back and not worry about having to sell it. (...) 2nd vehicle a co-worker found for us. Bought it from an *Autohaus*, paid cash! (...) Sold it privately two years later via Scout 24 [www.autoscout24.de]. 3rd vehicle: company car. Got hit big time on the taxes! (...) In spite of the cost, it is a very good deal."

Car dealers usually offer financing plans, ranging from 24 to 60 months, mostly requiring a down payment, or they offer a discount or lower interest rates if a down payment is made. Still, it is recommended to also check with your bank in case they can offer you a credit that is more advantageous than the car dealer's financing plan.

If you want a fairly new car without actually paying what you would have to pay for a new car, a good choice may be a *Jahreswagen* (cars that are bought by car manufacturer employees for a discounted price and sold after a year) or a *Vorführwagen* (cars that have been in the car dealer's display room and used for test drives). These cars tend to be in good condition and are far cheaper than a new car, as the prices for cars drop rapidly within the first year, even if they have hardly been driven.

Often, car dealers also offer to take care of the registration for you, which might be especially useful if you are not familiar with the German language or feel confused by the amount of red tape involved. I will give you some information about registration, insurance and mandatory inspections later on.

If you decide to buy a used car, most dealers give you some guarantee on it, but of course you will always find the odd black sheep. Private owners do not give you guarantees, the first thing to check on a used car is whether the TÜV is still valid. German cars have to be inspected by an independent agency, the TÜV, in regular intervals (usually every two years) and if they have major defects, the TÜV will not allow them to be driven anymore. Cars that are approved by the TÜV get a little plaque on the number plate showing when the next inspection is due.

When buying a car, make sure that you are handed out the *Zulassungsbescheinigung Teil 1* (previous name: *Fahrzeugschein*) as well as the *Zulassungsbescheinigung Teil 2* (previous name: *Fahrzeugbrief*). You always have to have the *Zulassungsbescheinigung Teil 1* with you when you drive as proof that you are allowed to drive that vehicle. The *Zulassungsbescheinigung Teil 2* should never be in the car, as this is legal proof of your right of ownership. It should be kept with your papers at home as you generally only need it when registering or selling your car.

If you want to make sure that the car you want to buy is in good condition, you can have it checked by the ADAC (German Automobile Club) or the TÜV. They charge you for the inspection but as they are independent, you can be confident of getting a good estimate of the car's condition.

iv) Registration, insurance and TÜV

Once you have bought a car, you need to have it insured as you are not allowed to drive it – and actually cannot register it – without proof of third party liability coverage for all damage or injury to another person, car or object. Of course you can have further insurance for your car and it is basically your decision how much coverage you want or can afford. As the insurance rates also depend on how many years you have driven accident-free, it might be advisable for you to get a certificate for a good diving record from the insurer in your home-country.

After you have insured your car you need to register it at the *Zulassungsstelle* (vehicle registry). As mentioned before this can usually be done by the car dealer. If you register the car yourself, you will need proof of ownership (generally the *Zulassungsbescheinigung Teil 1* and *Teil 2*) and proof of insurance as well as your passport. The car must also have a valid TÜV plaque. Then, your name and address will be added to the *Zulassungsbescheinigung Teil 1* and *Teil 2* and you will get your number plates. You will have to pay a fee of about € 50 for the whole process of registration and getting the number plates.

Once you have a car, be sure to not miss a TÜV inspection, as you can get fined when a policemen finds an outdated TÜV plaque on your car. Another regular – usually yearly – inspection is the ASU, which is a vehicle exhaust emission test. This can be done at the TÜV or most service garages. If it is passed, you get a plaque as well as a written certificate, which you should carry with you when driving. Going to the TÜV can be a time-consuming affair, but apart from that it is not complicated. (If you have the option to make an appointment via the internet, use it, because then the whole TÜV visit takes less than 30 minutes). You just drive there, present your vehicle documents (*Zulassungsbescheinigung Teil 1* and Teil 2) as well as the receipts from the last TÜV and ASU inspections (if applicable) and pay a fee. If you don't want to deal with the TÜV, you can bring your car to your car dealer or a garage and they take care of everything. They either take the car to the TÜV personally or have a TÜV employee pick up the car.

v) Automobile Clubs

If you drive frequently, it might be advisable to become a member of a German automobile club, the main one is the ADAC (Allgemeiner Deutscher Automobil-Club). For an annual fee of about 45 €, they offer emergency roadside service, an extensive selection of maps and travel guides, options for additional insurance and several other benefits. Their webpage (in German) offers further information and the possibility to sign up (www.adac.de).

Another automobile club is the AvD (Automobil-Club von Deutschland), basically offering the same services for a yearly fee of about € 59 (www.avd.de), and a third automobile club is the ACV (Automobil-Club Verkehr Bundesrepublik Deutschland) with a yearly fee of about € 60 (www.acv.de).

The emergency service can be invaluable if you have a breakdown, as a large part of the towing costs (if necessary) is covered and if you only have a small defect, the men from the automobile club can sometimes repair it right away or at least fix it so that you are able to drive home or to a service garage. On the side of the highways you will find emergency telephones at regular intervals. Check the little black arrows on the white posts next to the highway, as they direct you to the closest emergency phone. The phones are bright orange and you only need to open the flap at the front to get an immediate connection.

e. Traffic rules

Germans adhere strictly to traffic rules and traffic lights signals and you are well advised to do so as well, not only because of the high fines. So even if you don't have to take a written and/or driving test, you should familiarize yourself with the main traffic rules and signs. This website is a good point to start: www.gettingaroundgermany.info/auto.shtml. The website also covers all aspects of driving in Europe including renting, buying or shipping a car.

Also, good travel guides give you a first overview about German traffic laws. Here are a few points that might be different to the rules in your home country:

i)   Speed limit

> *"And at 180 km per hour (around 110mph) you're king of the road – for at least 30 seconds until that small black dot in your rear view mirror takes shape and blows past you doing >240kmph.. It's about the size of a bread box, and it goes fast, whatever it is."*

Many people think that Germans are rather aggressive drivers and you might likely get the same impression if you drive on German highways, the Autobahn. On many highways there is no speed limit at all, so it is not rare to see a large BMW or Mercedes overtake you on the very left lane at 220 km/h (which is about 140 mp/h). However, in the areas with speed limits, those are strictly enforced by a system of fines and points. If you are caught speeding you will have to pay a fine (sometimes on the spot but usually a ticket will be mailed to you) and if you exceed the speed limit by far, you will get points. Those points are collected in a central database and if you reach a certain amount of points, your driver's license will be taken away. Also, some offenses are punished by a prohibition to drive for a specified time, e.g. three months. If there are speed limits on the highways they are usually about 100 or 120 km/h; by rain the speed limit is 80 km/h. In the cities the speed limit is 50 km/h (by law, this is not specifically pointed out by signs) and in some areas (especially residential areas) it is 30 km/h. On large country roads it is 100 km/h, unless otherwise posted.

ii)   Overtaking
It is strictly forbidden to overtake cars from the right and when
you overtake (from the left!), be sure to check the rear mirror
and glance quickly over your left shoulder, as cars can
approach very quickly on the highways. Try to use the left
lanes on the highways only for overtaking (unless the right
lane is crowded with lorries).

iii)   Breakdowns
If you have a breakdown, try and get to the hard shoulder on
the very right of the highway or country road. Turn on your
hazard lights. If you have to get out of the car, be very careful,
especially on the highways. Many people have had accidents
darting out of the car after a breakdown. You have an
emergency triangle in your trunk (it is mandatory!) and you
should put this up on the hard shoulder about 200 m (600 ft.)
behind your car. Carry it in front of you while you walk the 200
m. Only after you have secured the area in this way should you
walk to the emergency phone or call for help on your mobile.

iv)   Good Samaritan Law
Be aware that in Germany there is a Good Samaritan Law,
meaning you must stop and help if you see an accident. If you
just drive on, you could be prosecuted for failure to give
assistance! If you don't know anything about First Aid, you
have to help as far as you can, even if it means just calling for
help on the phone and staying with the injured person.

v)   Alcohol
The blood alcohol limit is 0.5 per mill, as in most European
countries. If the police stops a car and has reason to believe
that the driver has consumed alcohol (usually due to the smell
of alcohol), they will ask the driver to be breathalized. They
cannot force the driver to undertake the breathalizing.
However, if the driver refuses to do so and if there are
justifiable grounds to suspect that the driver's alcohol level is
above the legal maximum, the police can force the driver to
undergo a blood test to determine the alcohol level. The same
applies if the breathalizer shows that the alcohol level is higher
than the legal maximum. This blood test may only be made by

a licensed doctor. The penalties for driving under the influence of alcohol are very strict.

vi) Seat Belt
It is mandatory to wear a seat belt, both in the front and back seats (the only exception is for back-seat-passengers of old cars that don't have seat belts installed in the rear). If a policeman sees someone driving without a seat belt (or passengers who don't wear a seat belt), they can stop the car and fine the driver immediately. Also, children under the age of twelve or smaller than 1,50 m (5 ft) are not allowed to travel in the front passenger seat and need to be secured in a special children's seat.

vii) Right of way
Generally – unless otherwise indicated – cars coming from the right have the right of way, this especially applies in residential areas. Be sure to familiarize yourself with the signs that give you the right of way, or indicate that you must yield the right of way. Busses pulling out from bus stops always have the right of way. As soon as you see a bus at a bus stop in front of you giving the signal to pull out, you must give them the right of way.

viii) Pedestrian crossings
If you see a pedestrian attempting to cross the street at a pedestrian crossing (they are called *Zebrastreifen* – zebra stripes – in Germany) you must stop to let them cross.

ix) *Feinstaubplakette* (Emissions control sticker)
Since January 2008, you may only drive in some German cities if you have a *Feinstaubplakette* on your windshield. These stickers can be picked up at the *Zulassungsstellen* for a small fee and are red, yellow or green, depending on the emissions rate of your car. It applies to most cities and more join continuously. You can inform yourself about the current status here: www.umweltbundesamt.de/en/topics/air/particulate-matter-pm10/low-emission-zones-in-germany.

f. Kirchensteuer (Church tax)

Germany is one of the few countries in the world that deducts church tax. When you start your employment in Germany, you will be asked whether you belong to either the Roman Catholic (*Römisch-Katholische*) or the Protestant (*Evangelische*) church. If you say that you belong to one of those churches, a church tax will be deducted from your salary every month. If you say that you do not belong to either church, you won't have to worry about church tax.

g. GEZ (Television fees)

If you are from the UK, you will be familiar with the system of having to pay a mandatory fee for the use of the television. Whereas private TV channels in Germany (just like everywhere else) finance themselves with commercials and competitions where you have to make expensive calls to win, there are also public TV channels here – the two main German channels ARD and ZDF and the regional programs of the Bundesländer. ARD and ZDF show commercials as well, but far less than the private channels and only at certain hours. An advantage is that they don't interrupt any of the programs as the private channels do. Whereas in the US public channels have fundraising events and shows, in Germany they are financed by mandatory fees (public radio channels are financed this way also). This means that every household has to pay this mandatory fee of currently 17,50 € per month.

If you want to have cable/satellite TV you have to pay an extra fee, depending on the package you book. In apartment buildings, cable TV is often included in the rent and you don't have to sign up for it. If it is not included you can ask your landlord, neighbors or colleagues where to sign up.

VI. Leisure and social life in germany

Germany has a rich social life and offers many possibilities to spend your leisure time in an enjoyable way. In the section about the 'German year' (page 92) you could already read about some of the special social occasions that take place throughout the year, but there is of course far more than that.

Once you have overcome the first obstacles of house hunting, dealing with bureaucracy and finding out how things work in Germany, you can start to discover your new home country. Partake in different leisure activities, maybe try out something you haven't done before, do sightseeing (all of Germany and its European neighbor countries are just a day or weekend trip away) and make new friends – Germans and other expats. This will greatly enrich your life in Germany.

1. Leisure in Germany

In the questionnaire I asked the expats if they noticed any social activities different from those in their home countries. Most said that the leisure activities were similar, but a few things were mentioned that expats noticed here.

a. German *Gemütlichkeit*

One was that board games were played a lot and that during parties people tended to sit and talk-more than to dance. It is true that Germans enjoy what they call "*Gemütlichkeit*" (coziness) and evenings when friends meet to play board games or watch videos/DVDs. I haven't been to many German parties where there was any or a lot of dancing and I never thought much about it until I lived in the US for a while. My friends there always danced at parties and at my first party after returning to Germany, I was surprised to see people just sitting and talking, even when really good music was being played.

Barbecuing (*Grillen*) in the summer is yet another popular aspect of *Gemütlichkeit*. Most people love to barbecue and if you are outside on a warm evening, you will most certainly notice the enticing smell of sausages, steaks etc. from an adjoining garden. Butcheries sell specially marinated pieces of meat for barbecuing, grilled potatoes and vegetables are also popular. People often invite friends over for evening barbecues.

This goes hand in hand with a German specialty – the *Schrebergärten*. *Schrebergärten* are little allotments of land that can be rented by people who don't have a garden where they live. These allotments are united into little colonies with certain rules and regulations, where people create their own individual little garden, often spending their whole free time in their own Schrebergarten.

b. Beer gardens and pubs

Several expats mentioned the beer gardens. As in many countries where good weather can't be taken for granted, people rush outside at the first glimpse of sunshine. During summer, beer gardens and outdoor cafés are extremely popular. Beer gardens are more common in the southern part of Germany and are part of the outdoor area belonging to a restaurant or café, bordered by trees, with special beer garden tables (long and narrow) and benches. They don't only serve beer, of course. In Hessen, you will find that apple wine (*Apfelwein*, or in the Hessian dialect: *Ebbelwoi*) is very popular, either pure or mixed with mineral water. In Bavaria the specialty is *Weißbier* (wheat beer). You also find a large selection of non-alcoholic beverages and wines as well as cakes and little snacks. I would say that generally the atmosphere in the beer gardens is more informal than anywhere else and due to the long tables, it is much easier to start a conversation with others sharing the table with you. Some beer gardens are in idyllic locations in small villages or in the middle of untouched nature and some also provide playgrounds for children.

Over the past few years, Irish and British pubs have become more and more popular in Germany and almost ever larger city features at least one such pub. They are very similar to the pubs you find in the United Kingdom or in Ireland, serving British or Irish food and beer and often having English or Irish waiters. Many English-speaking expats meet here and the atmosphere is relaxed and enjoyable.

c. Dining and wining

If you like to go out for dinner, you will enjoy Germany. There is an abundance of German and international restaurants and bars around, even small towns usually feature at least one Italian or Chinese restaurant. A short glimpse into the Yellow Pages for Frankfurt (which looks similar in every larger city) shows restaurants of the following cuisines: American, Arabic, Argentine, Australian, Austrian, the Balkans, Bohemian, Brazilian, Caribbean, Chinese, Croatian, Cuban, French, German, Greek, Indian, Irish, Italian, Japanese, Korean, Lebanese, Malay, Mexican, Persian, Portuguese, Spanish, South American, Thai, Turkish and Vietnam. If you ever miss the food from your home country, chances are likely that you will find a restaurant offering such food.

Typical German restaurants are characterized by the expressions "*gutbürgerliche Küche*" or "*gutbürgerliches Essen*", which basically means they have good plain cooking. If you yearn for some *Sauerkraut* or a *Schnitzel*, this is the place to go. Another indicator for good plain cooking is the word "*Brauhaus*" (brewery). These restaurants serve their own beer and a selection of local snacks and meals.

Apart from restaurants, you can also try out the less formal "*Imbisse*" – snack restaurants. The Italian version is called "*Pizzeria*", which is usually furnished with a few simple tables and chairs and offers basic, but good Italian food and a take-away option. German *Imbisse* often come in trailers and sell the general fast food – bratwurst, French fries or hamburgers. Turkish and Greek *Imbisse* feature Döner and Gyros, meat in a large pita bread with salad and sauce. Most *Imbisse* have a few tables for standing or sitting.

Of course the large fast food chains like McDonalds or Burger King found their way to Germany a long time ago. They look just like they do everywhere in the world and can be found everywhere.

Weinstuben (wine taverns) are usually in quaint old houses, often with a garden to sit in in the summer. They serve a good selection of wines as well as snacks and food, mostly good plain cooking. Hessen has the added specialty of applewine (*Apfelwein*) taverns.

Bistros and cafés serve smaller meals and often have tables outside as well. Some of them also serve quite good breakfasts until the early afternoon hours. Old-fashioned cafés are extremely comfortable and carry a large selection of self-made cakes and pastries. They have different coffee specialties and also often a larger selection of tea. They are perfect if you care for a pleasant time in homey surroundings and want to do some people-watching. A more modern version are Starbucks and similar coffee houses that are becoming popular in the larger cities.

Germany has many ice-cream parlors/ice cafés, most of them run by Italians. They are closed in the winter months when the rooms are used for selling other items, but in spring they open up again and serve an amazing selection of ice cream. You can take some in a cone or you can sit down and have one of the elaborate sundaes. The choice of sundaes becomes more refined and larger every year, there are special children's sundaes which are created to look like a bee, a bear or a mouse and there are sundaes with various kind of fruit, with alcohol or with refined compositions of nuts, crunchy sprinkles, chocolates, sauces and syrups for the adults. They are definitely worth trying!

If you go to a regular restaurant, tavern or café, you won't have to wait until you are seated. Usually, you can walk right in and sit wherever you like. If all the tables are taken and if you are in a less formal restaurant, you can also ask people at a table whether you can share the table with them. If you end up sharing a table with others, you are not required to strike up a conversation (remember – Germans are private and reserved), but sometimes they welcome it or they might strike up a conversation with you. Even if no real conversation takes place, it is seen as good behavior to wish the other party *"Guten Appetit"* ("Enjoy your meal.") when they receive their food and to say *"Danke"* when they wish you *"Guten Appetit"*. Whoever leaves the table first, says *"Auf Wiedersehen"* (Good bye) to the remaining party.

More exclusive restaurants usually require a reservation and when you enter the restaurant, you will be led to your reserved table. Even if you don't have a reservation, you should wait to be seated in such restaurants.

Some restaurants have English menus, so it is worth asking for one if you have received a German menu. However, restaurant staff does not always speak good English, although chances for this are higher in larger cities or where there are many tourists.

Often the bill is not brought to you unless you ask for it, as restaurants usually believe in not rushing their guests. When you get the bill, you always settle it with the waiter, there are no extra cash registers as you often find in the US. Tipping is not required, but if you are satisfied with the service, a tip is expected. However, the tip percentage is much lower that in the United States. With smaller bills, you just round up to the next full Euro (so when the bill is for € 7,60, you can round up to € 8,00). Otherwise a tip of about 5% is sufficient in most restaurants. You might want give a larger tip in exclusive restaurants, but never more than 10%.

d. Town festivals

Throughout the year, mainly in summer, many town festivals take place. Some cities and towns have their annual festivals that attract people from the surrounding areas, there are open-air music festivals, gourmet festivals, wine festivals, fairs etc. Larger cities also offer annual museum events or museum nights when most museums in the city are open to visitors free of charge and where there is a real party mood with food stalls and music. As these events usually take place in the city center you are advised to get there by public transport to avoid being stuck in a traffic jam or to discover that there are no empty parking lots. You can find information about festival dates in tourist information brochures, travel guides, websites or newspapers. Some international clubs also have regular bulletins that include information about events. – In winter, the Christmas markets (see page 95) are the main attraction.

e. Clubs

As mentioned already, Germany is a country of clubs. You can find clubs for almost everything – be it sports, needlework, reading, country dancing, breeding rabbits or playing cards. If your German is sufficient enough to get by with daily conversation, you might want to consider joining a club as it can be a good way to meet other people who share the same interests. Many international clubs also have their own sub-groups, so that you can join them even without language skills. The British Club of the Taunus for example has a book club, a group for mothers with small children, a bridge group and several other groups for their members.

You definitely won't have difficulty to find a German or international club of your interest.

f. *Spazieren gehen*

Just like the coffee and cake mentioned on page 95, going for a walk ("*spazieren gehen*") is a typical weekend and holiday tradition. As long as the weather is dry, many people will go out for a walk, either enjoying nature, discovering a new town or just going to their city center or taking a walk in the neighborhood. Maureen Chase pointed out that "there is more walking here with your family on the weekends. Everyone is out even in the cold weather." Often such a walk is combined with a rest in a beer garden (that is why some beer gardens are situated in the middle of the woods close to popular walking paths) or during cold weather in a cozy café.

g. *Stammtisch*-Culture

When asked about special German leisure activities, an expat from Australia pointed out the *Stammtisch*-culture. A *Stammtisch* is a table in a restaurant or pub that is reserved for a special group of regular customers. Some clubs or groups also call their regular meetings "*Stammtisch*". This, however, is something more usually found in the older generation and less popular among younger people.

h. Sports

Even small towns in Germany usually provide several provisions for sports, both indoors and outdoors. There are many lakes and outdoor pools, tennis courts, golf courses, football fields and of course you can hike and ski in many areas of Germany.

i. English cinemas, theaters and libraries

Large cities have a rich cultural life and they offer a wide selection of concerts, operas and theater plays to choose from. If your German skills are not sufficient to follow a German play or movie, you still don't have to do without these cultural amenities, as many larger cities feature English cinemas and theaters which attract expats and Germans alike.

Many international clubs also offer small libraries with English books and videos for their members, so it's always worth asking. You can also find English books in some of the larger public libraries in the big cities. Large bookshops usually have a section with English books and some cities and towns have special English bookshops.

2. Sightseeing

I strongly advise you to use your time in Germany to travel around the country as well as across the borders to the countries that adjoin Germany. Germany has the benefit of an excellent public transport, flight and highway system and you will probably be surprised how many wonderful attractions are within range of a day or weekend trip.

I don't intend to give you a full overview of German sightseeing here. It would definitely go way beyond the scope of this book and therefore I would advice you to revert to a travel guide or one of the travel websites I suggested. Local tourist information centers are always great resources (although sometimes only in German). However, I want to give you a summary of the main German attractions so that you know what the country holds in store for you. First, you can read about the regional sights in North, Middle, East and South Germany. Afterwards, I will give you an introduction of the themed tourist routes that provide an easy and convenient way to get to know the attractions that interest you most. Further sightseeing tips can also be found in the chapter on Germany's history.

a. North Germany

North Germany consists of the *Bundesländer* Schleswig-Holstein, Mecklenburg-Vorpommern, Niedersachsen and the free cities Hamburg and Bremen. It is the only part of the country that has a sea coast – there is the North Sea and the Baltic Sea. Both are lined with charming seaside resorts. Rügen and Usedom are the largest German islands; especially Rügen is famous. You can visit the well-known chalk mountains on the coast or enjoy the posh little resorts with their lovely hotels and mansions. Immediately south of the Baltic Coast lies the Mecklenburgische Seenplatte, a wide landscape with innumerable lakes, small quaint villages, nature parks and the occasional castle.

The North Sea coast is lined with several small islands as well, which are very attractive for those that like to hike, cycle or swim. Some of the coast islands do not permit any cars at all, for example Borkum, Juist or the small island for families – Baltrum. See the noble – and oldest – seaside resort Norderney or explore the islands Langeoog, Wangerooge, Föhr, Spiekeroog or the numerous others. The most exclusive island is Sylt, the island of the rich and famous. The backland features the famous Lüneburger Heide, a large area of heathland of exceptional natural beauty.

North Germany was largely dominated by the trading union *Hanse* (see page 34) and even today the old prosperous trading cities haven't lost their appeal. They shine with lovingly restored old city centers, impressive medieval residences or public buildings and have a special flair. Hamburg especially has always had a reputation of being extremely sophisticated (this is where you meet the most reserved Germans, by the way). Bremen is a little smaller and in my opinion somewhat lovelier. Further splendor can be seen in Lübeck, Flensburg, Rostock, Stralsund or Schwerin with its definitely noteworthy castle.

Go to the north of the county to enjoy its somewhat rough and very beautiful nature, the impressive trade cities and of course to eat freshly caught fish!

b. Central Germany

Central Germany, consisting of the *Bundesländer* Nordrhein-Westfalen, Hessen, Rheinland-Pfalz and the Saarland is an area of many contrasts. It has areas of great natural beauty with lovely towns full of half-timbered houses, notably the Eifel in the very west, the Taunus, north of Frankfurt and the Odenwald, south of Darmstadt. Also, one of Gremany's largest industrial areas is to be found in Central Germany – the Ruhrgebiet, northwest of Cologne and Düsseldorf. Just east of the Ruhrgebiet you find the Sauerland, a green and hilly area and the place where the *Ruhrgebiet* inhabitants like to spend their weekends.

Münster, north of the *Ruhrgebiet*, is a beautiful city with a remarkable history and a long-standing university tradition. It features wonderful medieval and renaissance buildings (all reconstructed after the city was destroyed in World War II) and is surrounded by the Münsterland where some of Germany's most beautiful moat castles are situated. One of these castles – Nordkirchen – is called the Versailles of Westfalen. If you like to cycle, you can take part in special cycling tours leading you to the different castles in the area.

Other highly recommended historical cities are Limburg in North and Fulda in East Hessen. The Limburg cathedral, a magnificent structure in bright colors, can even been seen from the highway A3 that passes Limburg. In the south-west corner of Central Germany lies the small Saarland with its capital Saarbrücken, where you can visit the impressive city castle that was built in the late 17th century. Koblenz, at the meeting point of the rivers Moselle and Rhine, also can pride itself of a history going back 2000 years.

You can use Koblenz as the starting (or finishing) point for a tour along the Rhine river. While driving directly along the river, you can see many picturesque villages that live mainly from wine and tourism. Vineyards cover most of the hills alongside the river and on top of some of the hills there are the famous Rhine castles, each one impressive and worth a visit. If you don't want to drive, you can also take boat tours up and down the Rhine.

Yet another facet of Central Germany are the elegant and culturally diverse cities of Köln (Cologne), Düsseldorf, Frankfurt or Wiesbaden. Köln has a lovely old center and the Cathedral is absolutely famous and should definitely be visited. Düsseldorf is more elegant, the old part is smaller but there is a nice area on the Rhine bank. Note than Köln and Düsseldorf entertain a kind of friendly rivalry, so many people from the area are either fans of Köln or Düsseldorf. While Köln is famous for it's Kölsch beer, the beer of Düsseldorf is the Alt. Don't order Kölsch in Düsseldorf or Alt in Köln!

Frankfurt was almost completely destroyed in World War II and so not many of its beautiful old buildings are left. Therefore, one cannot call Frankfurt a handsome city, but there are also still some very attractive areas here. Its internationality and its cultural diversity makes it especially attractive to expatriates. Wiesbaden is an old spa, which was popular with many crowned heads in the past centuries. Now it is still the place where you find impressive spa buildings and gardens as well as some exclusive shopping streets.

Central Germany is easily accessible, especially as several airports (the largest being the Frankfurt airport) are situated here. Come here to indulge in nature, do some major shopping or soak up history.

c. East Germany

East Germany encompasses the *Bundesländer* Brandenburg, Sachsen-Anhalt, Sachsen (Saxonia) and Thüringen (Thuringia) – most of what used to be the GDR until 1990. Not readily accessible for tourists until the reunification, it is now a remarkable destination, with many historical gems, especially in Sachsen and Thüringen.

Natural attractions are the Spreewald southwest of Berlin, home of the famous Spreewald pickles, the Thüringen Forest (Thüringer Wald) in the south of Thuringia with its mountains and rich forests or the *Sächsische Schweiz* in Sachsen.

Berlin and Leipzig are cities that combine the old and the modern. Smaller towns like Meißen, Wernigerode or Quedlinburg let history come alive with their amazingly restored half-timbered houses, classicist mansions and castles. Dresden and Erfurt are larger cities with remarkable splendor. Dresden with its many architectural treasures, has been reconstructed for many years after the reunification, as most of the city was destroyed in the terrible bombing of February 1945. It gives you a good impression of the prosperous and important city it was at the zenith of the Sachsen kingdom. Erfurt paints a vivid picture of a city in the late middle ages and the renaissance.

Weimar, a little town close to Erfurt used to be the center of German culture in the late 18th century, with great minds like Johann Wolfgang von Goethe and Friedrich Schiller, who lived and worked there (see page 41). It was also the location where the first republican constitution in Germany was established (see page 51) and in the dark years of the Nazi regime it became infamous as the location for the concentration camp Buchenwald, which can be visited today.

If you are interested in Goethe, Thüringen is the place to visit. Goethe spent most of his life here and several towns in the area were honored by his visit. Another highlight in Thüringen is the Wartburg that quite often played a role in German history (pages 41 & 44).

East Germany is pure history - the middle ages, the period of enlightenment, the Wilhelminian times, the short republic, the Nazi terror or the division and reunification of Germany. Combined with remarkable nature and extremely good bratwursts, it is definitely worth a visit.

d. South Germany

South Germany composes two of Germany's largest *Bundesländer* – Bayern (Bavaria) and Baden-Württemberg. Whereas the north of Germany is dominated by rougher nature and the population is known for its more reserved style, the south seems to flow over with baroque castles and churches and natural superlatives. Southern Bavaria with its bright green pastures and shining white Bavarian-style houses sometimes just look too idyllic to be true. The *Bodensee* (Lake Constance) is the second-largest lake in Western Europe. It is bordered by Germany, Austria and Switzerland and you find several little towns of outstanding beauty, well preserved and very historical, all around the lake. The south side of the *Bodensee* is bordered by the Alpes, which form a striking contrast to the large lake. The city of Konstanz on the south bank of the *Bodensee* has lived through a long and exciting history and presents many impressive old mansions as well as a fabulous view over the lake.

München (Munich), the capital of Bavaria, is well-known for its *Oktoberfest* and *Hofbräuhaus*, but there is more to the city. Parks, a wide and impressive old part of the city, museums and beer gardens have something to offer to every traveler. When in Munich, don't forget the Castle Nymphenburg, a beautiful example of baroque architecture. South-west of München you can visit Germany's most famous castle and the one that seems to grace every American travel company's Germany poster – Neuschwanstein. It is the most lavish castle that was built by

Bayern's legendary king Ludwig II shows an almost unsurpassed luxury. It lies on a mountain, surrounded by the spectacular nature of the Alpes. There are also several other castles built by Ludwig II., all of them unique and luxurious. One is just next to Neuschwanstein, called Hohenschwangau. Then there is Herrenchiemsee, which was to become a new Versailles, but was never completed.

You can tour many prosperous old cities with impressive castles all throughout South Germany. The best examples are Augsburg, Nürnberg (also famous for its Christmas market), Würzburg, Regensburg, Heidelberg and the small town Rothenburg o.d. Tauber, which is a well-preserved example of a late medieval town.

If you like to hike or climb mountains or eat a real Bavarian Weisswurst, if you enjoy history and magnificent architecture, South Germany is perfect for you.

e. Themed tourist routes

I personally think that the themed tourist routes in Germany are a wonderful idea. If you like fairy tales, you can get a map that guides you along the German fairy tale route to all the places that interest you. Several other tourist routes (more than 150!) with a variety of themes lead throughout Germany. You can order maps and then decide to travel along a complete route or discover just parts of one. Following is an introduction of the main tourist routes in Germany. You can find a more complete list of tourist routes at www.germany.travel/en/index.html (click on "Leisure and recreation" and then "Scenic Routes") or by looking for "Ferienstrassen" in the internet.

Burgenstraße (Castle route)

If you like castles, the castle route will be the thing for you. It is one of the longest tourist routes, over 975 km it leads from Mannheim to Prague (Czech Republic). Along the route you will get to see about seventy castles or castle ruins. There are also several nice old towns with medieval centers and the nature along this route is definitely worth seeing as well.
Further info: www.burgenstrasse.de (also in English)
Email: info@burgenstrasse.de

Deutsche Alleenstraße (German avenue route)
Throughout Germany, especially in the eastern parts, you can find long avenues leading through rural areas, lined with beautiful trees. It is enjoyable to drive along them and therefore the German avenue route has the intention to lead drivers along the most beautiful tree-lined avenues in Germany. Not all the avenues along this route are fully lined with trees so far, but it is the aim to get this completed soon. The route that leads through all of Germany from North to South.
Further info: www.alleenstrasse.com (also in English)
Email: info@alleenstrasse.com

Deutsche Alpenstraße (German Alpine route)
The oldest tourist route is the Deutsche Alpenstraße leading you along the lovely villages and towns that are located at the foot of the Alpes. The route is 460 km long and shows you great views of the Alpes and other nature attractions, small villages, spa towns and of course castles.
Further info: www.deutsche-alpenstrasse.de (also in English)
Email: info@deutsche-alpenstrasse.de

Deutsche Fachwerkstraße (German half-timbered houses route)
The Deutsche Fachwerkstraße stretches from the Black Forest up to Hamburg. Half-timbered houses were very common during the last centuries, so you will find innumerable towns everywhere in Germany with superbly renovated half-timbered houses. The route is divided into regional parts that are all connected to each other.
Further info: www.deutsche-fachwerkstrasse.de (also in English)
Email: info@deutsche-fachwerkstrasse.de

Deutsche Märchenstraße (German fairy tale route)
The Brothers Grimm are from Germany and their world-famous fairy tales all take place in Germany. The Deutsche Märchenstraße, (600 km long), takes you from Frankfurt to Bremen, leading you to all the towns, areas, museums and castles where the Brothers Grimm lived and worked, and

where the homes of some fairy tale characters are assumed to have been. Special events, taking place throughout the year, make the route even more interesting: fairy tales are staged, there are regional festivals and knight tournaments.
Further info: www.deutsche-maerchenstrasse.de (also in English)
Email: info@deutsche-maerchenstrasse.de

Deutsche Weinstrasse (German wine route)
This short (85 km) route leads you along the second largest winegrowing area in Germany, close to France. Enjoy the villages and vineyards, indulge in some wine tasting and visit the trails left from the times the Romans produced wine here. Apart from many castles, ruins, churches, parks and museums, you can see the world's only largest wine barrel (which is now actually a restaurant).
Further info: www.deutsche-weinstrasse.de (only in German)
Email: verein@deutsche-weinstrasse.de

Limesstraße (Limes route)
The Roman border wall, called Limes, stretched over 500 km (330 miles) from the Rhein to the Donau (see page 31). Today, only remains of this impressive wall can be seen, like ruins, towers and reconstructed parts. The Limesstrasse takes you along the Limes, pointing out the most important Roman findings and museums.
Further info: www.limesstrasse.de (also in English)
Email: limesstrasse@aalen.de

Romantische Straße (Romantic route)
The Romantic route lets you delve deeply into the opulent castle culture of Southern Germany. You will see large baroque residences, as well as Roman remains, medieval towns, richly decorated/ornamented churches and of course the charming nature of the surrounding area.
Further info: www.romantischestrasse.de (also in English)
Email: info@romantischestrasse.de

Route der Industriekultur (Route of industrial culture)
You get a different view of Germany on the route of industrial culture. It mainly takes you through the *Ruhrgebiet*. The route features several visitor centers and connects you with 150 years of industrial history. You can see old technical plants, museums, technical attractions and also villages that were built by the large industrial companies for their workers, with rows and rows of identical neat homes.
Further info: www.route-industriekultur.de (only in German)
Email: news@route-industriekultur.de

3. Meeting Germans and other Expats

Moving to a new area when one doesn't know anybody is always difficult, and an international move usually means overcoming the obstacle of a new language. It is already hard to meet people in general, but it can prove an almost impossible task with a language barrier. This is one of the reasons many expats stay within expat communities and make friends in international clubs or exclusively among expat colleagues. But wouldn't it be a pity if you returned to your home country after a few years without having made a single German friend? I always found it rewarding to make friends with people from different countries and cultures. It is fun getting to know the little cultural differences and learning more about my friends' home countries. I find my life to be much richer with these interesting international contacts. As living in another country for several years is one of the best ways to make international friends, I highly recommend you to try to make German friends during your stay in Germany. As mentioned before, this can also help you deal with culture shock and to understand cultural differences and the reasons behind them.

After reading about Germans being reserved, protecting their private life and separating social life and work, you might now have the impression that although it might be interesting to make German friends, it must be a problem to get to know anyone in the first place. The question of how, if at all, expats made friends was of course one of the main issues in my questionnaires. To my pleasant surprise, half of the people who replied stated that they didn't find it difficult to make German friends, and even those who did, eventually succeeded.

a. "It just takes a while."

Germans, apparently, take a long time to decide whether they like a person enough to become friends. An expat from the UK said it could take up to a year: "They scrutinize you for about a year before deciding whether you can be asked to do things with them. After they've decided to be friends you have fantastic friends for life but that first year is lonely."

If you read pages 74 - 78, you will know the reasons for the reserved conduct of many Germans and hopefully you will not understand it as a sign of dislike. I am sure that if you accept the fact that making friends in Germany can take some time, you will eventually be rewarded with many sincere friendships, as many expats confirmed in the questionnaires. I assume that people who invest a lot of time in establishing a friendship are interested in cultivating it afterwards.

In internationally influenced cities and environments people are often more open towards meeting other people, this also applies to Germans who join international clubs for the purpose of meeting people from other countries. Several expats reported that they made German friends through American or international clubs.

It definitely doesn't harm to sometimes take the initiative. A good time to start is when you are new in a city, you can ask colleagues or acquaintances whether they would mind showing you around. Maureen Chase gives another very good example for showing initiative in getting to know her German neighbors better by using a popular German "tool" - coffee and cake: "I have decided to invite my neighbors over for *Kaffee* and *Kuchen* sometime soon so I can get to know them better."

b. The language issue

As mentioned before, getting to know people who don't speak the same language as you can be difficult. If your new neighbor only speaks German and you only speak English, it is almost impossible to have a little neighborly chat. You will find that many Germans, especially the younger generation, speak English quite fluently. Nevertheless, several expats told me that they knew their lack of German was a major barrier to meeting Germans. As Robert Lederman says: "Friends were easy to make, we just didn't have a lot, because I spoke very poor (…) German. (…) Had I spoken good German, life would have been much easier. Neighbors and such were very friendly, but conversation was generally limited to 'Hi' and 'How are you?'"

Maureen Chase made the experience that so far, she only made German friends to whom she could talk to in English: "But our common language is English. I know the people on a casual basis in my building and they are really friendly, but I don't have too many German friends that I can speak with only in German, again because of my poor communication skills at the moment."

Getting to know others therefore can already be motivation for learning German. A further asset of having German-speaking friends is that you can practice your German skills, which will in turn help you with your daily life in Germany. Don't be afraid to use your German knowledge, even if you find it far from perfect. Most people all over the world greatly appreciate it if a foreigner tries to speak their language and Germans are no different in that respect. However, you might notice that many Germans will automatically talk English with you, even if you address them in German, simply because they assume you will be more comfortable with that. I have to admit I do that myself with English or American friends, mainly because I am not sure how much German they understand. So if you want to practice your German with native speakers, it can be helpful to tell them that you'd prefer to speak German. There is more about the attitude of Germans to non-German speakers on page 159.

c. Where to meet people

There are several places to get to know people – both Germans and expats. In my opinion, a good place to start is in one of the many international clubs. Just after you arrive in Germany, more than anything else, you are occupied with the battle of daily life, with language issues and just generally try to find your way around, so an international club where you meet people in the same situation can be an invaluable haven of security. About two-thirds of the respondents to my questionnaires stated that they had joined such a club and found much help and support there. Following are a few

comments from expats who joined international clubs:
- "The AWCT [American Women's Club of the Taunus] has been very helpful."
- "I enjoyed the info in the newsletter and of course the writer's club."
- "Very useful, lots of information and people 'in the same boat.'"
- "[The club] is a life-saver. Helps you get set up."

One expat also pointed out the English and international churches. In and around international cities like Frankfurt you can find various international churches of all religious denominations.

Language courses or special interest clubs can also be a good way to meet people with which you share an interest. If you have children, you can meet other parents at playgrounds, through playgroups, kindergartens and schools. You can send your children to a German school or kindergarten, but there are also several international schools in Germany (see www.internationalschools.net for details).

Some other places where expats met people were:
- "Sharing flats, talking to Germans in Irish pubs (they relax a bit there) and very slowly through work"
- "Work, Pubs."
- "Playgroups, through other English-speaking people."
- "Neighbors and people we meet through work."
- "Gym, my neighborhood, joined a volleyball team, my son's kindergarten, through my husband's work, German teachers."
- "At uni and at work."
- "We made most of my friends through my German classes. I did attend an English round table for a while."
- "I have met (...) two Germans through the Writer's Group. I also have two German friends through the (...) playgroup."
- "Sports club, language classes."

Maybe you were surprised to read that many expats met people through work, as I pointed out that Germans make a distinction between work and private life. Many of these expats work in international teams and so often most of their work colleagues are also expats. One expat told me that she found it hard to meet Germans because her husband worked in an all-expat office with English-speaking colleagues. But it is of course also possible to make German friends through work. As mentioned before it depends on the company culture and the area where you live and work. If you are working in Germany, I am sure that with some patience you can make good friends among your colleagues. If you have a spouse who is not working, it can also be a good idea to invite colleagues and their spouses to your home so that your spouse can also make new friends. – Many companies have Christmas parties or special department days/events where colleagues can talk to each other in a more informal setting, so parties and events like that can be very useful when you want to get to know colleagues better.

If you are not working, there are several other ways to meet people, as you can see from the above statements made by expats. Join an international club, take German lessons and if you like sports, join a gym or a sports club. If you like to go out, check out whether there are any pubs in your city, where you can meet people of all nationalities. You read that several expats mentioned their neighbors being friendly, so if you consider your neighbors nice people, just invite them over for some coffee and cake or a summer barbecue. Once you get out and if you are open to meeting people, you will quickly build up a good social network.

d. Some closing advice on social life in Germany from other expats

"Persevere – it takes time. Go to things that are international in character – they tend to attract Germans who are interested in foreign things."

"Be polite."

"I think one should find an activity one enjoys – art, ceramic, book club, hiking etc. – and join a group. You meet many wonderful people this way and have a good time doing it."

"Get out and enjoy it, experience it. Stay away from people from your own background and mingle with the locals if possible."

"Be patient – it takes longer to get to know people, however once you do they will be true friends."

"Enjoy it, learn the differences if any from your own culture. And, bring something like flowers or chocolate or a small gift if you are visiting someone in his or her home."

"Just be open to it."

"Without a good understanding of the German language, it is impossible to fully take advantage of the very strong and good German social life."

VII. Daily Life

Daily life in a new country can pose many hitherto unknown difficulties but it can also be an opportunity for interesting new experiences. You have the chance to discover a completely new shopping environment and discover all kinds of food that you have never even heard of before and which you might be interested in trying, or you will find that learning a new language can be a lot of fun. It can be a rewarding experience as well as a booster for your confidence to discover how easy life can be when you know the language. If you work, you will gradually discover little cultural differences at the work place and you might even get to like some of them.

It is always an advantage to have a general idea of what to expect when you are confronted with a new situation. I therefore asked expats about their daily life experience and will give you some information about important aspects – shopping, health care, learning and using German, financial matters, sending mail and working in Germany.

1. Shopping

a. General information

Apart from the shopping hours you will find shopping in Germany comparatively convenient. Basically, almost every town and city has a pedestrian area (Fußgängerzone) with all kinds of shops. Whereas the shopping areas in large cities basically all look the same and comprise many large department and chain stores, smaller towns often have unique little shops and boutiques. If you are looking for a nice present or tasteful home decoration, the smaller towns are often the best places to go to.

Many areas in Germany feature one or several large malls – they are still smaller than most American malls, but they offer a good blend of shops and plenty of parking space. Outlet malls are not that frequent yet, but are consistently expanding.

A good way to buy food is to go to the weekly markets that you find in almost every town, usually in the central market square. Farmers, butchers and other salesmen offer fresh vegetables, cheese, meat or spices for sale. There is always a good selection and although prices may be slightly higher than in the supermarkets, the quality is worth paying more. There are also farms that sell their produce directly, it is worth checking them out, especially if you value ecological cultivation and meat products from animal-friendly raised livestock.

Some larger cities also have food halls where farmers, fishermen etc. have regular stalls and sell their food during the regular shopping hours. You can find many exotic and foreign foods there, so if you are looking for food from your home country, this can be a good place to go.

By now, we also have some expat stores – usually in areas with a large expat community – to cater for expats who want to buy food or other items from home (these stores mainly have American and British items). There are also many online expat stores offering all kinds of things from "home". If you type "expat shopping" or something similar into an internet search machine, you will get countless examples. Some general expat websites (see page 8) also recommend or have links to online expat stores.

Although Germans were always willing to pay good money for good quality, and did not appreciate the flood of special offers and cheap stores, their attitude has changed a bit. due to the difficult economic situation. Discount supermarkets like Aldi, Lidl and Penny are now even popular with people who are better situated. There are also discount stores for electronics or clothes as well as "1 Euro shops" that are all getting more and more popular. Being thrifty doesn't have a negative touch to it anymore. Still, many people are now becoming more aware that many of these cheap stores not only treat their employees not well, but also get their good from suppliers which employ children and other poorly paid and treated workers in Asian countries. Food scandals and the awful treatment of livestock also brought some reality focus back into the "cheap is great" world. Some - unfortunately not enough - people now shop with more awareness. It also should come as no surprise that most of the bargain stores don't offer good quality. Special offers like "buy two for the price of one" that are familiar to many Americans are not as popular in Germany, so you will see them less often here.

There is a publisher who sells special voucher books in

several cities, including vouchers to use in certain restaurants, enabling you to order two meals but paying just for one (www.gutscheinbuch.de – only in German). Bonus programs like Payback (www.payback.de – only in German) or store customer cards have also found a good market, you can collect points when you shop at certain shops and later exchange the points for money, a voucher or a gift. By now you can hardly encounter a shop that doesn't ask you whether you collect "points", "hearts" or something similar, and the question *"Haben Sie schon unsere Kundenkarte"* ("Do you already have our customer card?") is also – sometimes annoying - standard by now.

When I came back to Germany from the US, I was used to paying almost everything by credit card. I had forgotten that although credit cards and bank cards were generally accepted methods of payment in Germany, a shop would often refuse payment by credit card if the purchased amount was under a certain limit e.g. 10 Euros. Smaller supermarkets usually don't accept credit cards at all, but would accept the bank card (see more about the bank card on page 163). It is better to pay for smaller purchases with cash.

Internet shopping is popular as well, even though many people don't use it because they are worried about transmitting their credit card or bank details over the net. Internet shopping here is subject to the same safety guidelines as in any other country.

b. Food shopping

"Not as much choice as I'm used to and although the supermarkets are open longer I still miss shopping on Sundays."

"It [food shopping] is very good, especially with the fresh market specialties. I wish the local supermarkets had bigger parking lots."

"It's a little different. I'm used to big supermarkets that stock everything, of which there aren't a lot here. Separate drug stores are a new concept for me!"

"German supermarkets are very old-fashioned with very little selection. In the UK, the supermarkets have a bigger selection and also cater for different nationalities."

"Total shock at first. Small stores, limited selection, poor hours, having to bring your own bags. (...) It was so hard to try and buy things over the counter, when you don't speak much German. Learned to do a lot of pointing."

Variety

Many expats commented on the limited selection in German supermarkets. I found this an interesting aspect as I personally never found the selection that limited. It shows that expats from other countries are apparently used to a much more varied selection. Supermarkets here are definitely smaller than those in America, for example. Even the shopping carts are smaller.

The variety you find also depends very much on where you go shopping. There are some large supermarkets (for example Real, Famila, Allkauf, Toom) that literally store everything from basic foods and drugstore items to TVs, clothing and small pieces of furniture – often on two floors. If you are looking for more exotic foods, it is advisable to go to the above mentioned stores, as they usually have a section for international food items, including specialties from Asian countries, Turkey, Greece, Russia etc. Often these large supermarket buildings also house several smaller stores like hairdressers, shoe repair shops, pharmacies and the like.

Then, there are the smaller supermarkets (for example Rewe, Plus, Kaufland, Edeka) that usually only carry food products and maybe a few drugstore items. You can get most regular food products you need for daily life here, but you won't find many special items.

Discounters like Aldi, Lidl or Penny have a more limited selection and usually not much variety in fresh produce. You can get all daily-food items there at a comparatively low price and sometimes they have special offers for clothes or electrical appliances, which are usually credited good quality.

Large department stores like Kaufhof often have food corners in their basement. You can find a good selection of international foods and specialities there, of course for a certain price. Also, the food halls are always a good place to go for a wider selection.

There are also several special stores, like bakeries,

butcheries or fish shops. Although Germans readily embrace the concept of the convenient supermarkets, they still prefer purchasing their bread and meat in special stores. Drugstore items are also usually purchased at drugstores and not in supermarkets. Organic food can be found in the *Reformhaus* and the *Bioladen*, which are dedicated to organic products, there are also organic supermarkets in most bigger cities (such as Alnatura or Denn's).

The lack of choice with regard to convenience and ready-to-serve food was also mentioned in the questionnaires. Germans don't really have a TV-dinner culture. There is a selection of instant meals, mainly pizzas and pasta dishes, but it is definitely limited in comparison to the variety in America and also far less popular.

Getting food from your home country

"Some cravings never went away."

One question in the questionnaire was whether the expats tried to buy food in Germany that was typical of their home country. Many replied that they had tried to buy such food and usually had succeeded quite easily. As mentioned before, most large supermarkets stock a certain selection of international food products. When I shopped for my first Thanksgiving dinner in Germany, I found everything I needed, including sweet potatoes, cranberries and pumpkin, right in the supermarket. As mentioned before, there are more and more international or expat shops opening up that stock special food products. Larger cities also feature Asian, Arabic or African stores. Here expats state where they found their favorite home-country foods:

- "There's a British shop in Köln, but I also found many of the Indian, Thai [and] African products I buy in Britain as well as some British products, like proper tea, in shops owned by non-Germans."
- "Grocery store, expat store."
- "Now popcorn, cranberries, Caesar salad dressing, barbecue sauce and lots more are readily available in the supermarkets that have a good selection. I still haven't

found graham cracker crumbs for pie crusts – but that's certainly no big deal. We still miss the good shrimps and T-bones."
- "Most grocery stores."
- "The expat supermarket or I bring them from home."
- "The internet."
- "At first we used to bring back from Canada suitcases full of stuff that we couldn't find in Germany, but over time I learned how to find replacements for everything."
- "I found them at Kaufhof in the basement."
- "There is an Australian shop that sells vegemite and tim-tams. There are lots of Asian groceries around, and the larger supermarkets stock the Mexican food I like. With a little bit of initial effort, raw ingredients are easy to work around."

Getting 'typical' German food

Some expats told me they had never tried to buy food products from their home country because they like the German food. Living in a new country can be a good chance to get to know other kinds of food and dishes that one learns to like. German meals by far surpass the *Sauerkraut*, *Knödel* and *Würste* for which the country has apparently become famous.

Typical food dishes vary from region to region. In northern Germany you can find an abundance of fish and other seafood dishes. The south of Germany features dishes similar to the ones mentioned in the previous paragraph. Potatoes are popular everywhere and served in several different ways – boiled, fried, as potato fritters etc. etc.

Apart from regional specialties, German bread is always commented upon favorably by Germans and non-Germans alike. Germany has about 300 different kinds of bread, from soft white bread to the darkest pumpernickel. You will find bread made from all kinds of different flour, with grains added or covered with oatmeal. The small "version" of bread are the rolls (*Brötchen*), the selection of which is comparable to the assortment of bread.

German chocolate is also a must! Again, you have a great variety – white chocolate, milk chocolate, dark chocolate, some with delicious fillings like strawberry cream, nuts, toffee cream, nougat or marzipan. Another chocolaty delicacy you will soon discover is the chocolate bread spread. Although it originated in Italy, it is extremely popular in Germany.

If you like beer, try out the more than 5,000 (!) different brands of German beer. It is comparatively strong compared to the American beer. Every German region has its own typical beer, among the most famous are the Kölsch from Köln and the Weißbier from Bavaria.

The intricacies of food shopping in Germany

"I wish they had personnel to pack the groceries. That can be a stress if people are waiting behind you in line. I think it's pretty ridiculous that you pay extra for a plastic bag when buying groceries, since you get plastic bags free with everything else you buy."[1]

"I keep forgetting to bring along a [Euro] for the Wagenpfand, so would have to stand in line for change. I also wound up with a huge stash of bags at home because I never remembered to bring them along."

"You have to bring a bag with you and not get too much at once if you live in the city and don't have a car. I don't like having to rush rush after the groceries are checked and get them in my bag, kinda stressful, BUT I find the lines move quicker here in the grocery stores, so the rush rush at the end is worth it. Just getting used to it."

If you want an example of what many non-Germans would call a lack of customer service, come to a German supermarket. However, most Germans don't consider the general conduct in German supermarkets as a lack of customer service, but rather helpful in speeding up the shopping process. This German shopping culture can come as a shock to many expats from countries where groceries are packed for them and where they

---

[1] Note that since 2016 this has changed - most supermarkets only sell paper bags and most other stores have started to charge for their bags. The very good and valid reason is a heightened awareness of the environmental difficulties of plastic and the attempt to therefore reduce plastic.

can get as many free plastic bags as they like with their groceries.

The shopping culture shock can even start before you enter the store. You can only get a shopping cart if you insert one Euro (sometimes, you can also use a fifty-cent or two-Euro-coin) as a deposit. Shopping carts are locked to each other and the deposit opens this lock. Instead of a Euro you can also use special plastic chips that have the same shape as the Euro. Therefore, you always have to make sure that you carry a Euro coin with you. I keep my coin in my car, not in my purse. You will probably forget to make sure that you always have a coin the first times you go shopping, but you get used to it quickly. Bonnie Barski doesn't mind the deposit and says: "The Euro deposit to get a grocery cart is a good idea. That way shopping carts aren't scattered all over the place like they are sometimes in the States."

The first section in the supermarket usually is the fresh produce section. There, the second potential pitfall awaits you. In some German grocery stores or supermarkets, you have to weigh any loose produce you buy yourself before you take it to the cash register. To find out whether weighing is necessary, look at the price tags. If you read the word *"Stück"*, you don't need to weigh them, as they are charged by piece not by weight. Indications that the produce is charged by weight are the abbreviations "kg" (*Kilogramm*) or "g" (*Gramm*). There are scales in the produce area that have several buttons displaying the different kinds of produce (if there are no scales available, or just a regular one without buttons, you can assume that you don't have to weigh the produce yourself, as the cashier will do it). Once you have made your selection, you place it on the scales and push the button that corresponds with the item on the scales. A price sticker emerges which you stick on your respective purchase. The only difficulty may be distinguishing between the different produce buttons. Some have only a word description or number while others have illustrations. As some people (Germans and non-Germans alike) tend to forget to weigh their produce, many stores, especially the larger ones, now have similar devices in the area of the cash registers, so that when you check out and haven't weighed all your produce, you don't have to run through the whole store. Still, as this of course holds up the check out process, it is better not to forget to weigh the items in the first place.

I recommend you always bring your own bag(s) to the supermarket. You can get bags at the supermarket, but they cost money. Many supermarkets now also sell reusable cloth bags. I use a shopping basket, which I find very practical, even for heavy items, and I always have a couple of cloth bags for any additional purchases I may make.

German supermarket cashiers have to be able to scan a certain number of products per minute over the cash register. The exact number can differ from store to store, but it is an impressive number in any case and most cashiers fully live up to the expectations. However, you won't be able to watch helpful supermarket personnel packing your groceries, you have to do that yourself, and it can get stressful. The best advice is to just put everything back into the shopping cart and then find a quiet spot to pack everything into your bags. Some supermarkets have special packing areas for their customers, at other supermarkets you will see customers drive their full shopping carts to their cars, where they put their purchases into bags. Aldi cashiers are supposed to be the quickest ones and from my experience I fully believe that. The speed definitely takes getting used to and even then it can be a little exhausting, but you'll be pleasantly surprised at how quickly check-out lines move.

2. Health Care

"[It was] easy to get in to see Doctors. All speak English."
"It used to be reasonable. Now it's gotten expensive."
"Very good [experiences]. And I even had a baby, all in German."
"Health care is very top notch!"
"My husband is being treated for kidney stones and I have to say his caregiver, and his department there, is giving him extremely good and attentive care. We are pleased."
"The service is pretty good, with respect to what you need for referrals, and the duties a GP can perform on the spot."

Most expats said that their impression of German health care was positive. There is no doubt that if you choose the right doctor, you can get excellent treatment in Germany. However, the type of insurance a person has can influence the quality of treatment he receives.

a. Health insurance system

In Germany, health insurance is mandatory. There are two main kinds of health insurance – public and private. Germans have to be insured via the public system unless they are self-employed or earn more than a certain amount of money per annum. The current (2017) minimum annual (gross) salary that allows an employee to get private health insurance is € 57.600. The minimum limit is raised yearly, corresponding to the rise in wages. Basically, employees earning less than € 57.600 per annum have to have public health insurance, whereas employees with a gross annual salary of € 57.600 or more can choose between the public health insurance and the private health insurance. If an employee's salary is reduced or he/she becomes redundant, the right to have private health insurance is lost (with a few exceptions).

If you are in Germany on an international assignment, you might anyway have an international health insurance, or an insurance in your home country that covers medical treatment in Germany. In that case, you will generally be treated as if you have a private insurance. If you work in Germany and are health insured here via your company, the laws regarding health insurance apply to you.

The premium/contribution for public health insurance is deducted from your monthly salary; a certain percentage is used for health insurance coverage, half of which is paid by you (via the deduction) and half by your employer. If you have a public health insurance, your spouse and children (as long as they are under a certain age and don't earn their own money) are also covered at no extra charge. This makes public health insurance attractive for families with children. There are several public health insurance companies and their rates vary somewhat. However, they all have to grant the same benefits, so that there is generally no difference in the amount of costs taken over by the public health insurances, as they are governed by a legal code, which lists all costs that are taken over for certain benefits. The flexibility of health insurance companies can differ to some extent regarding various matters (in some cases, the insurance company has discretionary powers as to whether it takes over coverage for certain treatment), customer-friendliness is also an issue. (However, the list of treatments covered is reduced from year to year and many people by now wonder why they pay huge insurance premiums if they also have to pay for many treatments themselves. The costs for glasses and contact lenses are not covered anymore, medication that is obtainable without a prescription cannot be prescribed anymore. Even if you get a prescription (as all doctors now have a prescription budget, you might not get a prescription simply because the doctor used up his budget for the quarter), you still have to pay a prescription fee when you get your medication at the pharmacy.

When you have a public health insurance, you get a chip card that has your relevant personal data (address, date of birth etc.) stored on it. You give this card to the doctor's receptionist every time you go to a new doctor or once during each quarter if you see the same doctor. The doctor settles his account directly with the health insurance company, you don't receive a bill.

Private health insurances have rates that are calculated from many factors – your age at the time you enter the insurance, your state of health (if you have chronic illnesses like allergies, asthma, thyroid issues etc., it can substantially increase your monthly premium, as I know from own experience) and even whether you are a man or a woman. Generally it can be said that a well-earning young healthy male in his late twenties or early thirties, who hardly ever goes to the doctor except for a yearly check-up can make a real bargain on his private health insurance premiums compared to the public health insurance premiums, which depend on the salary, while a woman in her late thirties with a history of allergies can be charged relatively high premiums. Another point to keep in mind (which is only applicable to you if you want to stay in Germany long-term or for ever) is that premiums get higher and higher in the advancing years which leaves some senior citizens with incredibly expensive insurance premiums.

However, one can also choose the kind of coverage one wants to have. Unlike the public health insurance, private insurances are not by law obliged to cover a certain range of treatments. The customer can choose whether he wants to include a dental plan, a single bedroom during hospital stays or alternative healing methods. All of these decisions influence the premium costs, so if you don't care for a single bedroom in the hospital, you can save some money if you go for a plan that doesn't include this option. Another option to save on monthly premiums is the so-called Eigenanteil, meaning that you carry part of the costs for treatments yourself, as for example 250 € per year, and only get reimbursements for costs exceeding those 250 €. Yet another way to save money is taking part in the incentive programs many insurances offer – if you get a yearly check up at the dentist, the amounts reimbursed for dental treatment can be raised yearly or if you are not overweight, a bit of your premium can be reduced if you can prove that your weight is stable for a while. These incentives differ from insurance to insurance.

People with private health insurance also receive a chip card. However, although you still have to present this when visiting the doctor, you will receive bills for treatment rendered (this also applies to international health insurance). You have to settle these bills with the doctor and then send them to your insurance for reimbursement (together with a filled out form, which is provided by your insurance). It depends on the insurance how quickly you get your reimbursement; my health insurance transfers the money to me within one to two weeks, which is not bad. If you have many bills or bills with high amounts, you should be aware that you have to pay them first and then wait for reimbursement, which could take a while. Most insurance companies ask you not to send in bills until you can get a reimbursement total of at least 100 €.

Persons privately insured are exempt from paying the fees on prescriptions. Furthermore, the doctor does not have a limited budget for prescriptions. However, you have to be aware that the insurance will not reimburse any doctors' bills that appear incorrect, so if you have the impression that your bill could be too high, you can send it to your insurance to be checked before you pay it. – When you hand in your prescription for the necessary medication at the pharmacy, you need to pay the complete amount straightaway and then send the prescription to the insurance for reimbursement, just like you do with the doctor's bills.

Regardless of whether you are insured publicly, privately or through your home country, you always have to show proof of some kind of health insurance when seeing a doctor. One of the first things you will be asked is to present your *Versicherungskarte*, which is your insurance chip card. Be sure to always have it with you.

b. Prescriptions and medication

"They [doctors] seem very willing to prescribe medication without trying anything else and keen to do lots of tests, which struck me as excessive."

"Doctors are less inclined to distribute antibiotics, but on the other hand American doctors dispense it like candy machines! On the other hand....I was very ill when I first arrived with bronchitis and a sinus infection and I needed antibiotics and I had to go to another doctor, other than my first one, because the first one did not give me antibiotics. (...) I wish there was a happy medium."

If you have a prescription, you have to get the prescribed medication at the pharmacy, the *Apotheke*. There are no drug dispensing counters in drugstores or supermarkets in Germany, the *Apotheke* is the only place to get prescribed medication. When I had to get medication in the US, I was very surprised when the lady at the counter told me that there would be a 25-minute-waiting period. Later, I learned that in the US, the pills are counted and filled into a container/bottle which is then labeled with the name of the drug, the patient's name and address as well as the dosage. You won't find that in Germany. Medications come in packets, usually in three sizes. Your doctor will always prescribe a specific size; for example "N1" means that you get the prescribed drugs in the smallest sized packet. Therefore, when you go to the pharmacy, the pharmacist just takes the prescribed size packet from one of the shelves or drawers and hands it to you. If they don't have the drug you need in store, they order it and it usually arrives within a few hours.

The German Pharmaceuticals Law is much stricter than for example American law. Therefore, it's possible that a drug that you can get over the counter in the US would require a prescription in Germany. Prescriptions in Germany do not include refills, so every time you need a certain drug, you have to get a new prescription (although if the doctor knows you well, it is possible to just phone and ask for a new prescription, which you can then pick up or have sent to you without having to make a new appointment).

You will also find that even over-the-counter medication can only be bought at the pharmacy. You won't find painkillers or allergy remedies in the drugstore or supermarket. Drugstores and supermarkets are only allowed to sell vitamin supplements or remedies on natural or plant basis like Valerian drops etc.

Pharmacies are usually open between 8.00 or 9.00 am and 6.00 and 8 pm on weekdays, some close during lunch time, usually between 1.00 pm and 3 pm. On Saturdays, pharmacies are usually open from 8.00 or 9.00 am to 12.00 pm. There is always one pharmacy in the area that is open in the evenings and on Sundays/holidays. Pharmacies on emergency service (Notdienst) are listed in the shop windows or doors as well as in the local newspaper (it is a rotating system).

If you or a member of your family requires a certain medication regularly, you should make sure that you can get this medication in Germany and if not, take a sufficient supply with you.

c. Finding an English-speaking doctor and making an appointment

Some of the questionnaire respondents mentioned that they never specifically tried to find an English-speaking doctor, either because they spoke sufficient German already or because they discovered that many German doctors spoke English.

Those who did try to find an English-speaking doctor reported that it was no problem (most expats live in or near big cities. If you live in the country or near a small town, it might not be so easy). The main sources were by word of mouth from friends, through international clubs or colleagues or the embassies, which usually have a list of English-speaking doctors. Some just looked in the Yellow Pages (Gelbe Seiten) and asked whether the doctor spoke English. Also, certain relocation agencies can provide you with a list of doctors, it's usually the same list that you can get from an embassy. You can also obtain such lists from the International Association for Medical Assistance (IAMAT). The IAMAT requires people to sign up as members and whereas membership is free, a donation is encouraged (www.iamat.org)

Generally it is advisable to make an appointment to visit a doctor, otherwise you might have to wait a very long time or you are asked to come back another time (unless it is an emergency or you are suffering any pain). Even if you make an appointment, it does not mean that you will not have to wait, during busy hours it is possible that you may have to wait up to an hour. It is advisable when making an appointment, to ask the doctor's receptionist when it would be best to come. You can also phone before leaving home and ask whether you will have to wait and then you can coordinate you time accordingly.

You do not need to register with a GP and you can switch to another doctor if you don't want to stay with the first one.

d. Emergencies and Medical Treatment outside Consultation Hours

If you need medical care outside consultation hours there are several ways of obtaining it. You can find the doctors on emergency duty by looking in your local newspaper under Notdienst, they are usually listed according to their special field. In most areas in Germany (except for Baden-Württemberg and parts of Hessen) there is now one central number for the Notdienst: 116 117. (Please bear in mind that you will probably not be able to request a specialist, as doctors on emergency call are on a rotating basis).

If you phone your own doctor outside consultation hours, you will get an answering machine message giving you the number for emergencies (unfortunately, this message will be in German).

You can also always go to a hospital or, if you are not able to get there by yourself, call 112, which is actually the fire department, but they provide an ambulance service in emergencies, and this would be the main emergency number. For police emergencies, the number is 110.

3. "Did you try to learn German?" – "Absolutely!"

On the previous pages of this book I often stressed the vital importance of learning German. This facilitates social contacts, daily life matters and to a certain degree also reduces culture shock (although knowing the language doesn't automatically mean knowing the culture; still, it is imperative for a better understanding).

German is not an easy language to learn, but nobody expects you to master it to absolute perfection. If you learn to get by on a daily basis, you will face day-to-day life in Germany with much more confidence and security. Every single one of the questionnaire respondents wrote that they either already knew some German before coming to live in Germany or they started to learn it after they had settled in. When asked to evaluate their skills, the replies covered every level between fluent and very basic, which of course also depended on how long the German lessons had taken place. After a few months of learning, skills were generally evaluated as good enough to get along relatively well in daily life. If you enjoy learning a new language and take every opportunity to practice it (watching German TV or reading German newspapers and magazines is a great help), you will probably find it much easier to learn than you expect.

The best time to start learning German is the moment you know you will be moving to Germany. The more you already know when you arrive, the easier the transition will be for you.

a. Where to Learn German

The options for learning German are manifold and there is a learning method to suit everyone's taste and budget. If you come to Germany in the course of an intercompany transfer or via university, you will probably be allocated a certain amount of German lessons in a language school, with a tutor or with special courses at university. Unfortunately, companies and Universities often don't include accompanying spouses in this offer, which I consider absolutely unacceptable. So, maybe when you come to live here, you will need to find a cost-effective method of acquiring the required language skills.

When I asked the expats where they learned German, they answered as follows:

- "Self[-taught], night school for the written word."
- "Language school."
- "At the university in the States and the Johann Wolfgang Goethe University in Frankfurt."
- "Language courses at the Goethe Institut and private lessons at home."
- "Uni, course and self-learning."
- "Plan on using a tutor one or two times a week. Took twelve or so private tutor lessons prior to arrival."

Language schools

Language schools and self-teaching courses were among the most popular methods. There are some well-known language schools in Germany, like Berlitz (www.berlitz.de – the Germany website is only in German) and Inlingua (www.inlingua.de – also in English) and their courses vary from large groups, which is the cheaper option, to one-to-one lessons, which are correspondingly more expensive. The benefit of these schools is that they are located all over Germany and are also reputed for their high standards. This is, however, one of the most expensive methods of learning German (maybe apart from a private tutor) and are therefore interesting for expats whose language courses are funded by their company.

There are also many not so well-known language schools in almost every town/city, the quality and prices of which can of course vary. Here, recommendation by word of mouth is a very valuable way of choosing a school. You will also find that international clubs often have members who give private lessons in German.

A less expensive, but not necessarily efficient method is adult evening classes, the *Volkshochschule* (VHS). The VHS offers courses ranging from needlework, yoga and belly dancing to a variety of languages. The groups there are larger, which makes the courses comparatively cheap, but the language courses usually don't give you the in-depth knowledge of a language that you need in daily life. As the groups are so large, you will also be together with people that have different skill levels and of course the course has to orientate itself on the person with the least knowledge. So, the VHS might be a good option for beginners, especially as you get to meet other people there, but you should accompany it with a self-teaching course or later switch to a language school. You can find a list of all German VHS and their courses at www.vhs.de.

Self-teaching courses
There are various kinds of self-teaching courses to choose from. However, from my experience with this kind of course, I doubt whether one can really learn a language from scratch. Again, this is my personal experience, so feel free to inform me if I'm wrong. The good thing about CD-ROM, online or app courses is that they sometimes come with a pronunciation test. The program gives you words or sentences that you need to speak into a microphone, which is attached to the computer and the program then rates your pronunciation. Some programs also offer small dialogues where you talk to the computer, the success of the exercise depending on how well the program understands you. In my opinion, those methods are very helpful to improve pronunciation. Videos and games add more fun to the learning experience. I would definitely recommend such a course as an addition to another learning method or to improve basic skills of a language.

The benefits of self-teaching courses are their price (compared to the more expensive language schools), the flexible timing (as you can decide when you do your studying) and their availability to those that live in area where there are no language schools. Still, they are only recommendable to those who can muster up the time and discipline to sit down regularly with the material and who are able to learn easily on their own. They have the disadvantage of not giving you the opportunity to meet other people and there is no teacher who can correct mistakes or answer any questions.

Goethe Institut
The Goethe Institute gives German lessons for several levels, takes exams and they have their own materials for learning German. There is also the chance for chats and forums. The high reputation of the Goethe-Institute guarantees good

German lessons.

The Goethe Institut is expensive, but it has an excellent reputation and is always a good choice. The institute also offers distance learning courses which are popular with people who have to travel much on business and can't attend a regular course.   Check out their course and material offers at www.goethe.de (also in English).

Universities

If you come to Germany on an international program, a German course is often included anyway. Apart from that, most universities offer several programs and courses for foreign students to learn German or to improve already existing language knowledge. These courses are sometimes also offered to non-students, so if you live in a large city with a university, you might want to check out their German lessons as well. Of course, they usually cost a fee.

b.   Germans' attitudes towards non-German speakers

People in most countries are delighted if foreigners try to speak their language, no matter how imperfect it might be. If they themselves know the foreigner's language well, they will often assist him by switching to his language. As English is such a universal language, people who speak it well will usually not get into the predicament of traveling to or living in a country where nobody understands them. However, it cannot always be assumed that everybody everywhere knows English. I remember my first journey to Hungary. I was so used to talking English while I was in other countries that I tried to talk English to everybody (on my first visit I didn't know any Hungarian at all). It turned out that hardly anybody there spoke English, in fact I got along far better with German.

When you move to Germany, chances are that you will probably sooner or later get into a situation where you won't be understood unless you talk some German. I asked expats if they had any experience with the attitude Germans had towards non-German speakers. As I work in an international environment and live in Germany's most multi-national city – Frankfurt – I always had the impression that Germans were open towards people who spoke only a little or no German at all. However, since I looked at the issue from a German perspective I was interested to hear what expats would have to say. I wanted to know whether they found that Germans were willing and able to speak the expat's native language and whether they felt that Germans were open towards non-German speakers.

- "I think they're all willing [to speak English], but some of the older people didn't learn it or are out of practice. The young people seem to almost all speak it."
- "Many people speak English, but people mostly are very appreciative when you try German and encourage you to do so."
- "Germans are so good at speaking English, and ask me if I'd like to speak English if I'm struggling, which is considerate, considering that I am a guest in their country."

All expats replied that according to their experience most Germans (especially the younger generation) knew English very well (incidentally, all expats who answered the questionnaires came from English-speaking countries) and were always very willing to speak it. One expat never tried to speak English to Germans as his German was so good that nobody realized he was from the UK. Some reported that Germans even replied in English when they were addressed in German.

In my opinion, when Germans know a language well, they enjoy speaking it and will use every chance to practice it. Mastering other languages is something many Germans are proud of and something they appreciate in others as well.

The replies on whether Germans were open towards non-German speakers were mixed. Some pointed out an issue which I can confirm – Germans are usually open towards people whose native language is English (probably because English is such a universal language and often used in the world of business), but it is a different matter with people who speak other languages. A sad but true fact is that expats who come from countries like the US, the UK, Australia or Canada might find that Germans are more tolerant towards them than people who come from Turkey, Morocco, China or Eastern European countries. Some answers to my question "Do you feel that

Germans are open to non-German speakers?" were as follows:
- "I enjoyed working there [in Germany] and was treated well as I spoke good German – my colleagues who didn't had a much tougher time."
- "Yes, very much so."
- "Some are."
- "It depends on where they come from – English: yes."
- "Yes. Germans are international."
- "I guess it depends on the language, and the German speaker in question. Like all people, I think they appreciate it when you try to speak the language of the host country."
- "Generally, yes. They are very tolerant."

As you can see, you won't normally have much difficulty or discover a lack of acceptance if your German is far from perfect. Still, it is equally obvious that even a basic knowledge of German combined with the willingness to use it, can make life much more pleasant. Don't be shy when you consider your German far from perfect. Your effort to speak it will always be appreciated and commented upon positively.

4. Banks

a. Opening a Bank Account

If you are staying in Germany for a longer period, it is convenient – or even necessary – for you to open a German bank account, as most payments involving large sums entail transferring money from or to your bank account. I will give you an overview of the different payment methods later on.

There are many different banks in Germany and most of them offer basically the same main services, even though their fees can differ, so make sure to compare fees. It could also be helpful to choose a bank that has a branch near your apartment or your office as their opening hours are not very convenient. They are usually open on weekdays from 8.30 am to 4 p.m. (some are open until 5.30 pm or 6 pm on special weekdays, often Tuesdays and/or Thursdays) and closed on weekends. Some branches (especially smaller ones) are closed during lunch-time. ATMs (*Geldautomat*) and internet banking make it possible to take care of most banking matters outside branch hours.

In order to open up a bank account, you need your passport and money for the initial deposit (you can also transfer money from another account but be aware that the transfer might take some time). Some banks will also require you to show a valid residence permit and proof that you are employed in Germany (e.g. written confirmation from your employer), so it is advisable to take these documents along as well. Generally, you will want to open a *Girokonto* (checking account) for which you receive a Eurocard (*EC-Karte*), which enables you to withdraw money from ATMs (not only in Germany but also in most other countries), to get bank statements from the machine and also to make payments, as it is accepted as a means of payment in most shops, gas stations, hotels, restaurants etc.; in fact throughout Germany it is more widely accepted than credit cards. To enable you to withdraw money and to pay in shops with the card, you will need a PIN number, which you have to apply for and which will then be mailed to you.

In Germany you can get money from your bank's ATMs without having to pay a fee and usually you can also use the ATMs of certain other banks without having to pay a fee either. You will usually find a sticker at the ATM detailing when a fee has to be paid for a withdrawal.

When opening your account you can agree on an overdraft limit (*Dispositionskredit* or just *Dispo*), usually up to a maximum to two or three times your monthly pay. Some banks might only allow this after a period of a few months, during which regular salary payments have been made to your account.

If you want a German credit card you might also have to apply for it at your bank, as some credit cards (e.g. VISA) are not issued by independent companies but only by banks. If you get a credit card via your bank, the credit card payments are usually automatically deducted from your account each month.

You can also get checks but this is not recommended, because as of January 1, 2002 they are no longer guaranteed by banks (before, they were guaranteed up to DM 400) and are therefore hardly accepted anywhere. Checks have never been a popular means of payment in Germany and will most probably, in future, cease to be used altogether.

Nowadays, most banks offer internet banking, which allows you to handle money transfers by computer and also to get bank statements online, it might be a viable option to you. You have to apply for it at the bank and depending on which system the bank uses, they will send you the necessary software or just the web page address. You will always get a PIN number and a list of transaction numbers, which you use for each financial transaction you make. Some banks charge you lower fees if you decide to use online banking.

There are banks where everything is done online or per mail. These banks are called *Direktbanken* and as they don't have so many offices, they are usually much cheaper and a real alternative to people who are comfortable with doing things online and don't necessarily need a bank contact person all the time (of course, you can contact people at these *Direktbanken* as well, but just per mail or phone).

b. Methods of Payment

Generally, people pay in cash for smaller purchases and you will discover that shops in Germany are not very willing to accept credit cards or EC-cards for small amounts, most shops have a set minimum limit for the use of these cards.

Paying with the EC-card is very easy. It's just like paying with a credit card. Sometimes, you have to confirm the transaction with your signature, sometimes you have to type your PIN number in a machine or you might even be required to show some personal identification.

Credit cards are accepted in most large shops and hotels, as well as in many restaurants, gas stations or train stations. Still, they are far less accepted than e.g. in the US, not all supermarkets accept credit cards.

Payments for rent, utilities, mail-orders etc. are made via the bank account, there are three major ways:

- Money transfer (*Überweisung*): money is transferred from your bank account to another bank account. In order to make the transfer, you have to fill out a form (*Überweisungsformular*). If you pay for a mail order or utilities, you will receive the form, already partly filled out, together with the bill from the company that receives the money. If you are not provided with a form, you can get blank forms at your bank. Of course you can also do these transfers online.

You can send these forms to your bank, put them directly in their own letter box or in a box inside the building during office hours. The forms have a carbon copy that you should keep for your own files. – Money transfers can also be made via online banking.

- Standing order (*Dauerauftrag*): this is useful if you have recurring payments for the same amount, e.g. your rent. You have to go to the bank to arrange for a standing order (or do it online) and then the payment will automatically be transferred from your account on an agreed date and at the agreed intervals.

- Direct debit (*Lastschrift*): you authorize a company to deduct payments directly from your account, i.e. for phone bills, utilities, or some mail orders. This authorization is called Einzugsermächtigung. You can cancel it at anytime and also revoke any payments deducted from your account within 90 days if they are incorrect. Direct debit is convenient if you have recurring payments with changing amounts, so that a standing order would not not feasible in such cases, but you should be cautious who you authorize to debit your account in this way.

5. The Postal Service

The German Postal Service is called *Deutsche Post*. Many branches also sell stationery and greeting cards, and if you have an account with the Deutsche Postbank you are able to make use of the integrated banking facilities. Larger post offices are open from 8 am – 6 pm, however smaller branches tend to close over the lunch hours and earlier in the afternoon, which, if you work regular hours, makes it almost impossible to do something as simple as picking up a parcel during the week. Saturday mornings are therefore usually very busy, so be prepared for a long wait! On the other hand many airports and main railway stations have post offices that are open 24 hours a day. Nowadays the Post Office also has contracts with several stationery /office supply shops, so – especially in smaller towns – you will not have a post office but an area in the shop with a counter, where postal matters are handled.

a. Postal Charges for mail within Germany

Standard Letter / *Standardbrief*   0,70 €
Length   from 140 mm up to 235 mm
Width   from 90 mm up to 125 mm
Height   up to 5 mm
Weight   up to 20 g

Compact Letter / *Kompaktbrief*   0,85 €
Length   from 100 mm up to 235 mm
Width   from 70 mm up to 125 mm
Height   up to 10 mm
Weight   up to 20 g

Large Letter/*Großbrief*   1,45 €
Length   from 100 mm up to 353 mm
Width   from 70 mm up to 250 mm
Height   up to 50 mm
Weight   up to 1000 g

Maxi Letter / *Maxibrief*   2,60 €
Length   from 100 mm up to 353 mm
Width   from 70 mm up to 250 mm
Height   up to 50 mm
Weight   up to 1.000 g

Postcard / *Postkarte*   0,45 €
Length   from 140 mm up to 140 mm
Width   from 90 mm up to 90 mm

b. Stamps

Although the Euro is the mutual currency most European countries, the use of stamps is a national matter. Stamps issued in Germany can only be used for letters sent within Germany or from Germany to another country.

Outside of most post offices you will find postage stamp

machines (*Briefmarkenautomat*). Many of these machines have computerized displays (usually also available in English) and built-in measurement guides so you can determine the correct postal charge for your letter according to size and destination. Keep an eye on the measurements because if the letter doesn't fit the measurements, higher postage may apply even if the weight is low.

If you order items from a catalog or return filled-out questionnaires or applications to companies, they usually provide you either with postcards to fill out or envelopes already printed with the return address. You do not have to put a stamp on such postcards or envelopes as long as there is the word "*Antwort*" (reply) printed above the address of the recipient. This means that the recipient has already paid the postage.

c. Post Boxes

You can recognize German post boxes easily by their yellow color. Unfortunately the *Deutsche Post* took down many of their post boxes for cost-saving reasons, so it can sometimes be a bit of a hassle to actually find one. The collection times are displayed on the box itself. You should be aware that some post boxes have two separate letter boxes. Over the left box you will see two postal/zip codes, e.g. 60000 – 60899 and on the right box you will usually read "*andere Postleitzahlen*" ("other postal / zip codes"). The left box is for letters with a local postal / zip-code and the right one for letters that are sent further afield – i.e. the postal / zip-code doesn't correspond with the two codes indicated on the left box.

6. Working

"Tough economy, stiff competition and better (of course) if you speak fluent German."

If you decide you want to work in Germany or change companies here, there are a few things you need to know.

Hardly any of the accompanying spouses who filled out my questionnaire worked in Germany (only on a freelance basis or together with self-employed husbands), which doesn't come as a surprise. If you read the section on work permit regulations, you will remember that unless you are from an EU-country or married to a German citizen, it is not easy to get a work permit in Germany.

a. Finding employment in Germany

The first thing you need to do is to find a job, which can be a challenge. If you don't know the language well, this of course poses an additional difficulty. However, there are always companies that specifically look for people who are native speakers in French or English with adverts in that specific language. The following suggestions are mainly aimed at those who speak German fluently enough to work in a German-speaking environment.

The internet features various job websites, for special professions or working fields (e.g. engineers, hotel employees or lawyers), for positions nationwide as well as on an international level and in all sectors. These sites are usually no different from the job websites you know from your home country. Sometimes it's possible to search for adverts in a chosen language, making it easier for you to specifically look for adverts in English. You can, alternatively, put your CV on the internet for potential employers to read and let them send you any adequate offers per email. The largest general job websites in Germany are:

- www.jobpilot.de
- www.monster.de
- www.stepstone.de

You can of course also go to one of the websites from your home country and search for jobs in Germany there, as many have international job ads as well, and you might feel more comfortable with an English-speaking website. Still, the selection for German jobs is definitely better on German websites. Another option is to look on expat websites, such as

- www.expatica.com/de/jobs
- www.toytowngermany.com/jobs/

If you are interested in a specific company, you can just check out their website. Some companies don't advertise in newspapers or on the general job websites anymore, but put any job vacancies on their company website. Even if a company that you would like to work for doesn't have a vacancy for a special position at that time, it doesn't hurt to send them an unsolicited application. If they find your background interesting, they might keep your CV on file until a suitable position is vacant.

The newspaper is also still a good way to find employment. Every town and city has a daily newspaper, in which you will find the most job ads on Saturdays. Some newspapers allow you to subscribe only for their Saturday editions, which makes sense if you are mainly interested only in the job ads. Local newspapers generally have ads for jobs where not much experience or education is required, so if you are looking for a challenging position on a higher level, you should look in the more reputed regional or the national newspapers (FAZ, Zeit, Süddeutsche Zeitung). Most newspapers also have their job ads on their websites.

Headhunters and job placement agencies have many contacts and if your job profile corresponds to their clientele of companies, they might be interested in your CV and keep it for further reference until a company shows interest in someone with your background. This method is best if you are qualified for a high-level managerial or specialist position.

One of the expats who answered my questionnaire chose to sign up with a temp agency (*Zeitarbeitsfirma*). This has the advantage that you can work in several different companies, therefore having better chances of finding a company you like. Usually the agency will find time-limited jobs for you, as a temporary replacement for regular employees who are on vacation or ill, or only for a specific task (if the company in question doesn't want to hire someone permanently).

Sometimes, temping for a company can result in a regular employment contract.

Temp agencies usually pay less than regular jobs, so this is something you should be aware of. They have a ranking system depending both on your background and on the job they send you to, which also influences your salary. Your employment contract is with the temp agency, so even if they don't find a job for you, they will have to pay you. Therefore, they are only inclined to make a contract with you and pay you a salary after they found work for you, which is why it is recommendable to register with several temp agencies. You are entitled to full employment benefits when you have an employment contract with a temp agency (make sure that it's a reputable agency).

Most temp agencies specialize in certain job sectors, so if you are interested in an administrative position, you should first find out which temp agency specializes in that sector. You will find job ads from temp agencies on the general job websites in the internet as well as on the agencies' own websites. Of course, you can also make an unsolicited application for a job, as they will put your CV on file and contact you when they find something adequate for you.

The employment agency (Arbeitsamt, now: *Bundesagentur für Arbeit*) also offers help with the job search. They have a website for job search as well, but unfortunately, it isn't very user-friendly. If you have worked in Germany and lost your job, you have to contact the *Bundesagentur für Arbeit* in order to get your unemployment benefit.

Don't underestimate networking, especially as an expat. International clubs or online expat associations often have special groups for working members and/or organize regular get-togethers for professional networking.

It is best to choose a combination of the methods mentioned above. Finding employment in Germany takes perseverance and effort, and is next to being impossible if you have language problems and the need to apply for a work permit. As one of the expats put it when I asked whether she considered finding a job in Germany easy for expats she replied: "As an English teacher, yes. Otherwise, no way!"

b. Applying for a job

Let's assume you find a job advert that arouses your interest or you know a company that you want to contact on your own initiative. After learning a little about Germany, you will probably not be surprised to hear that applying for a job here is a more formal matter than, for example, in the US.

It is different when you apply via email or maybe even via an electronic application form over the internet. In those cases, only a cover letter (which should not be less formal or meticulous than a hardcopy letter!) and a CV need to be attached, even though you can of course attach scans of other documents. If the company you apply to likes your cover letter and CV, they will most likely contact you and ask you to send them your complete application papers by post.

Generally, your complete job application papers (*Bewerbungsunterlagen*) should consist of the following:

• A cover letter
• A photo
• Your CV
• All diplomas from your high-school diploma to any university degrees
• Reference letters from previous employers
• Confirmation of any language courses (not the "Spanish for your next vacation" course, but certificates confirming a good knowledge of a foreign language) or job-relevant trainings (including courses for special computer programs like Excel or job-related seminars)

Apart from the cover letter, all these papers should be neatly put into a folder (there are special folders for job applications, although any nice folder will do), sorted into the above-mentioned categories and, within the categories, in chronological order.

i) Cover letter

The cover letter is probably not much different from the cover letters you write in your home country. It should not be longer than one page (recruiters or personnel managers usually just skim these letters), but stress your strongest qualifications, as it can decide on whether the potential employer will even look at the other documents or not.

Information that you definitely must include are:
- where you saw the respective job ad (of course this only applies if you are responding to a specific job ad)
- the position you are applying for (this can be put in the reference line above the letter text)
- a short overview of your previous work experience and qualifications
- why you find this job/this company so interesting that you want to apply
- what makes you a good candidate for the job in question (or for the company)
- one or two sentences about your language and computer skills

If applicants are requested to state the earliest starting date and/or their salary wishes, they should not omit this. If this is not asked for the information is not necessarily required, though a mentioning of the starting date can be useful.

If your CV indicates times of unemployment you can explain the reasons for this in your cover letter or mention that you would like to explain personally. You should of course have good reasons for such work interruptions, as you will be asked about them in every interview.

Be sure to make no spelling mistakes in your letter. If you are not sure about the fluency of your German, have a native speaker proofread your letter. This cover letter is the first impression your potential employer has of you, so make sure it looks perfect.

ii) Photo

A passport-sized photo should always be included. Generally, it's better to have photos taken by a professional photographer instead of using a photo machine. (I have to admit that I have always included machine-made photos with my job applications and it has never seemed to be a problem, but generally, it might be a good investment to go to a photographer). It goes without saying that you should not send a snapshot from your last vacation where you are sitting in a beach café in a tank top (before you ask: yes, I received job applications with such photos) or where you are wearing your most comfortable leisure outfit. A photo of you in a business suit / costume or at least wearing a nice top with a jacket is a much better choice (this is assuming you apply for office jobs).

The photo can be attached to your cover letter or CV with a paper clip or with glue, or scanned and inserted on the CV.

iii) CV

An American friend of mine once asked me to proofread her CV some years ago. I told her that she got it all wrong as she listed her most recent position first and then went back chronologically. Little did I know back then that this is how American CVs are written. At that time I had only been familiar with German CVs. By now, the American style is starting to be used here as well. It is, however, still not as common as the German style. Here, CVs are written chronologically, starting with your school education, any further education and work experience, concluding with the most recent work experience.

You should beging your CV, which by the way in German is called *Lebenslauf*, with your personal data. A career objective paragraph is not included. Don't mention your career objective in the CV. That should be stated in the cover letter in the explanation of why you are applying for the job in question. The following personal data is absolutely necessary in the CV:

• Name
• Address
• Phone number
• Email address
• Date of birth

If you are not German I would advise you to also mention your nationality and whether you have a work permit.

Then you should list your relevant education and work experience. If you have had several years of relevant work experience, I personally wouldn't recommend mentioning every two-week-internship or summer job you had during your school and university years, unless it is vitally related to the job you are applying for or it was a long-term position. If you are a university graduate, however such things should be included, especially as it is looked upon favorably if an applicant gained some practical work experience during his or her studies. – I now list the work I did during my university time under a special heading. Then I have a separate heading for my work experience after university graduation. Everybody handles matters like this in a different way, so you should estimate for yourself what you consider vital information. You can also find sample CVs on the web or ask your German friends to let you have a look at theirs.

Language and computer skills as well as any other experience (volunteer work, being involved in an association that is related to your work) should be included at the end of the CV. Some people also include their interests and hobbies. Again, this is a matter of personal preference.

Don't end up with a CV that spans several pages. Two pages should be a good length for you if you have already had some work experience. As a university graduate, one page might do. Just like the cover letter, the CV also is usually only first skimmed, so the person reviewing your application won't be pleased to find himself confronted with a five-page CV.

iv) Diplomas

Every graduation should be verified by a diploma. You will probably not have diplomas in German, so you might want to think about having them translated. If your diplomas are in English I don't think a translation would be necessary. I always include my American diplomas without a translation and nobody has ever asked me for one. However, if you have diplomas in languages that are less widely known I strongly recommend attaching a verified translation.

v) Reference letters

When you leave your current job in Germany, you are entitled to a reference letter (*Zeugnis*) from your employer (see more about this on page 183). Every potential future employer in Germany will want to see reference letters from previous employers. As such written references are not customary in many countries, you might not be able to include any. If you leave your home country and already know that you will be looking for employment in Germany, it is advisable to ask your last employer(s) for a reference letter. Basically, it needs to contain information about your position/function in the

company, your tasks, the duration of your employment there
and an assessment of your work.

If you are not able to get a written reference letter from
previous employers, you should explain this in your job
application. Most German HR people are aware of this
situation and are understanding. If possible, at least include
contact information of former employers, so that the potential
German employer can get some feedback from them if he wants
to.

c. Relevant Employment Law

I already gave a short overview of some points of
employment law (*Arbeitsrecht*) on the previous pages. In this
section I want to inform you about further aspects of
employment law that will be of interest to you if you work in
Germany. This overview is by no means complete and is not
intended as legal advice, but purely for informational purposes.
You can get a good impression of how complex this subject
actually is from the long list of legal codes and agreements
below that found the basis of employment law. Here, I just
want to touch upon a few issues that might be relevant to you
in the course of your working life in Germany. If you do
encounter an employment law problem or conflict, you are
strongly advised to contact a lawyer specialized in matters of
this subject.

The necessity of a work permit and information about the
process for obtaining one have already been given on page 99.

i) Legal basis

German Employment Law is based on several legal codes and
agreements, the main ones being:
- BGB ("Bürgerliches Gesetzbuch" – Civil Code) - Regulates
  the contesting of the employment contract (§§ 119 – 124)
  and the basic principles of the working relationship (§§ 611
  – 630)
- ArbZG ("Arbeitszeitgesetz" – Law regulating working
  hours)
- ArgGG ("Arbeitsgerichtsgesetz" – Law regulating the
  structure and procedure of the court for labor disputes)
- BetrVG ("Betriebsverfassungsgesetz" – Statute governing

workers representation)
- BurlG ("Bundesurlaubsgesetz" – Law regulating vacation)
- EFZG ("Entgeltforzahlungsgesetz" – Law about the payment of wages on holidays and during sickness)
- JarbSchG ("Jugendarbeitschutzgesetz" – Law to protect youths")
- KSchG ("Kündigungsschutzgesetz" – Law protecting against unjust dismissal)
- MuSchG & BErzGG("Mutterschutzgesetz" & "Bundeserziehungs-geldgesetz"– Law to protect working mothers and pregnant employees)
- NachwG ("Nachweisgesetz" – Notification law)
- SchwbG ("Schwerbehindertengesetz" – Law regulating working relationships of severely handicapped employees)
- TzBfG ("Teilzeit- und Befristungsgesetz" – Law about part time work and time limits on employment contracts)
- Collective bargaining agreements
- Works agreements
- Individual employment contracts
- Court decisions

ii) General principles
The regulations of the individual employment contract overrule the regulations of the legal codes, unless these contractual deviations are to the disadvantage of the employee. A deviation from the law to the disadvantage of the employee is never allowed, not even with the employee's consent!

The workers council (*Betriebsrat*) is the elected representative of all employees in the company. It is elected in companies which have a minimum of five permanent employees having the right to vote (employees over 18 years, no executives). It is not mandatory to have a workers council. If the company has one, it has to be heard before certain proceedings, members of the workers council also have a special dismissal protection among other rights. The rights and duties of the workers council are regulated in the *Betriebsverfassungsgesetz.*

There are two main sections of Employment Law – individual employment law (*Individualarbeitsrecht*) and collective employment law (*Kollektivarbeitsrecht*). The first regulates the contract relationship between employer and employee and will therefore probably be the only section that will affect you. The latter deals with workers councils, unions and similar collective rights and organizations.

iii) Probationary period (*Probezeit*)

Most employment relationships in Germany start with a probationary period of three months (mainly for menial jobs or jobs at a subordinate level) to six months. If you have been assigned to work in Germany for the same company as in your home country, the *Probezeit* will usually not apply to you, as its purpose is to find out whether the employee is competent and compatible (or vice versa) and to facilitate separation if the case is otherwise.

The *Probezeit* features all duties and entitlements of a regular employment relationship, with two exceptions. Firstly, an employee in the *Probezeit* is not entitled to dismissal protection to the same extent as regular employees. During the *Probezeit*, the notice period is just two weeks and no special reason for dismissal needs to be given. Secondly, full vacation entitlement only comes into effect after successful completion of the *Probezeit*, which means that although you are entitled to the regular number of vacation days during the trial period, you cannot actually take any vacation until after the *Probezeit* (sometimes, an employer will be generous and allow you to take a few days, but as the purpose of the *Probezeit* is to determine the compatibility of the relationship, the employee should refrain from taking time off beforehand).

iv) Salary deductions

Your employment contract will state a gross salary. As in other countries, certain deductions are made, mainly for social security and taxes. A rule of thumb estimation is that your net salary amount will be about 60 % of your gross salary. The following is a short overview of the most common deductions, so you will understand you payslip better:

• Wages tax – *Lohnsteuer*
• Church tax – *Kirchensteuer* (only if you say that you belong to either the Catholic or Protestant church)
• Solidarity surcharge – *Solidaritätszuschlag*

- Pension insurance – *Rentenversicherung*
- Unemployment insurance – *Arbeitslosenversicherung*
- Health insurance – *Krankenversicherung*
- Nursing Insurance – *Pflegeversicherung*

Note that if you are privately health insured, no deductions will be made for health and nursing insurance. Instead, you will actually get an additional payment, which is the employer's contribution to your health and nursing insurance. When you are publicly health insured, your employer pays the employer's and employee's share (which is deducted from your gross salary) directly to the insurance. However, when you are privately insured, the insurance collects the whole amount from you directly, which is why your employer pays out his share to you.

It is possible that you are exempt from having to contribute to all of these social security insurance schemes. Many countries have entered into agreements stating that a national from one country can continue participating in his home social security system instead of having to contribute to the host country's social security system. In such cases, your company needs to apply for a document that certifies this exemption. As agreements between various countries differ, make sure to ask your home or host country's HR or payroll department to see to it that you stay in your home social security system whenever possible.

If you are not exempt from unemployment insurance, you can get a reimbursement for the payments you made during your stay in Germany. This can be applied for at least two years after you left Germany. Make sure to clarify this with your German HR department before you leave Germany, so that you know what you will have to do to claim reimbursement from the German state.

v) Part time

Employees are entitled to part time under the following conditions:

- the employment relationship with the current employer has been in effect for more than six months
- the employer has more than 15 employees (not including apprentices/trainees)

The salary is of course reduced accordingly. It can be advisable to have the new gross and net salary recalculated, as a lower gross salary can get you in a better tax bracket and so reduce your deductions. However, if you are privately health insured, you should make sure that your new gross salary is not less than the minimum annual gross salary allowing employees to get private health insurance.

If you want to work part time, you have to make a request for this three months at the latest before the desired part time start date. In the request, you should state how you want to organize your working hours (for example, if you want to work 32 hours per week, you should clarify whether that means eight hours full from Monday – Thursday excluding Friday, or whether you want to work reduced hours from Monday – Friday).

The employer cannot deny this request unless there are important company-related reasons against it. These reasons have to be defined and justified clearly, e.g. a major disruption of organizational processes, endangerment of security or being the cause for significant additional costs are considered valid reasons for denying a request for part time work. The employer has to specify these company-related reasons one month at the latest before the desired part time start date. If the employer does not keep this deadline, the request for working part-time is considered agreed on.

Should the employer be able to state valid reasons for denying a request, a new request can be made at the earliest two years later.

If you discover after a while, that the reason for you wanting to go on part-time has become irrelevant, you have the right to go back on full time.

vi) The protection of pregnant employees and working mothers

The German constitution has a clause that states "Every mother is entitled to the protection and care of the community." (*"Jede Mutter hat Anspruch auf den Schutz und die Fürsorge der Gemeinschaft."*, Art. 6 IV GG). In order to comply with this constitutional obligation, also in the area of employment law, the *Mutterschutzgesetz* (Law to protect working mothers and pregnant employees) and the *Bundeserziehungsgeldgesetz* (Law for educational allowance) have been incorporated. Its aims are to protect working mothers from dangers to life and health at the workplace or resulting from work, from suffering monetary losses resulting from pregnancy and raising small children and from the loss of employment.

Women who are pregnant or nursing have to be provided with a work environment and conditions that don't damage their health. This means that they are exempt from doing tiring or dangerous work, they must be allowed to have breaks and be provided with seating facilities. If a continuation of the work is dangerous for the health and life of a pregnant mother and/or her unborn child, the woman must be released from work, but continues to receive her salary (the average salary of the previous three months).

A pregnant woman generally is freed from working six weeks before the anticipated birth date of their child as well as eight weeks after the child's birth (*Mutterschutzfrist*). She will receive a daily allowance from her health insurance and (if the health insurance's payment is lower than the net income) an additional payment from her employer.

Women cannot be dismissed earlier than four months after her child's birth, except in very special cases. This also applies to women who are still in the probationary period. The woman herself can quit her job.

After the birth of a baby, mothers as well as fathers are entitled to take unpaid parental leave (*Elternzeit*) up to three years. Parents can take this *Elternzeit* together or take turns. Generally the three-year period starts from the day of the child's birth and ends on the child's third birthday. It is however possible (as long as the employer agrees) to take the third year at a later date, between the child's third and eighth birthday. The employee has to make the request for *Elternzeit* in writing, addressed to the employer, in which she must specify exactly when she wishes to take leave (stating specific dates!). Generally, the request has to be made six (if the *Elternzeit* starts straight after the child's birth or the *Mutterschutzfrist*) or eight (all other cases) weeks before the desired start date of the *Elternzeit* at the latest.

During the *Elternzeit* the employee does not have to work and will not get a salary. The employee cannot be dismissed during this period. The *Elternzeit* can also be taken in combination with doing part-time work, that means instead of not working at all, the employee taking *Elternzeit* can work up to 30 hours a week. Both parents can choose this option, each one of them can then work up to 30 hours a week. The general regulations regarding part time apply.

Parents during *Elternzeit* are entitled to receive a tax-free daily allowance, called educational allowance (Erziehungsgeld) if they make a written request to the authorities (which differs from Bundesland to Bundesland, so you should contact your local authorities for information on the applicable authority) and fulfill the following requirements:
- the employee lives in Germany (foreigners need a valid residence permit!),
- takes care of the child in person,
- has legal custody of the child and
- does not work, or works part time up to 30 hours per week

However, if both parents fulfill these conditions, only one of them receives the Erziehungsgeld. It is only paid as of the ninth week after the child's birth, as the mother receives the daily allowance mentioned above up to that time. The Erziehungsgeld is reduced on a step by step basis if the parent's income lies over a certain minimum.

vii) Continuation of salary payments during sickness

If you are not able to work due to illness, you keep your wage claim for six weeks, if you are not responsible for the illness. Afterwards you have a claim for sick pay (80% of the wage). Sometimes health insurances or employers might ask for proof of work inability due to illness. You are obliged to undertake everything to accelerate your recovery. Failure to comply with this obligation can result in a reduction of salary.

Only employees whose employment relationship has been in effect for at least four weeks without interruption have salary continuation entitlement.

viii) Warning notice (*Abmahnung*)

The warning notice is an official warning issued by the employer when an employee does not fulfill his contractual obligations. This warning indicates that there has been a violation of contract and reminds the employee of his duties. Above all, it justifies dismissal at a later date, if that proves to be necessary. If repeated warnings fail to be successful, it justifies the employer to dismiss the employee without notice and to write an unfavorable reference letter. A warning notice is usually in writing (although it isn't compulsory) and kept in the employees file, even though it may only be kept for a limited time.

The warning notice must clearly state the violation of contract (general terms like "being unreliable" are not sufficient) and must include an order for improved behavior on behalf of the employee as well as the announcement that repeated violations justify termination of the employment relationship. In such a case, the workers council does not need to be heard.

The employee has the right to raise an objection to the warning notice. Regardless of whether the warning notice is justified, the employee can write a counter statement that must be stored in his files.

He can also demand that the warning notice be removed from his files and revoked if it was unjustified. A warning noticed is considered unjustified if any of the following cases apply:

- It is based on untrue facts or assumptions (including the assumption that a behavior constitutes a violation if in truth it does not)
- It is based on facts than cannot be proven in front of a court
- It is not commensurable (for example, the violation is much too insignificant to justify a warning notice)
- It includes formulations that are exaggerated, unobjective or insulting
- The employer has no further interest in keeping the warning notice in the files

The employer is the one who has to prove the justification of the warning notice.

ix) Dismissals

A dismissal needs to fulfill several formal requirements to be effective. A dismissal is null and void if the workers council isn't heard beforehand (this of course only applies to companies that have a workers council). The protest of the workers council against the dismissal however has no effect on the employer's decision, the workers council only has the right to be heard, but not to take action.

The dismissal must be made in writing (an email is not sufficient!) and signed. This also applies to a notice letter written by the employee. It is important that the other party receives the document. Although this sounds easy enough, there has been a myriad of court cases dealing with the question of whether a notice letter was received by the other party (generally the employee).

Sometimes it can be beneficial to both parties to end an employment relationship with a written agreement/ cancellation contract, which in German is called Aufhebungsvertrag. Generally, when both parties want to end the employment relationship without application of the notice periods, they choose this method. This can be in the interest of the employee if he has a long notice period, but has found a new position with a starting date that requires him to leave his current position much sooner. The Aufhebungsvertrag is also often concluded when a company wants to dismiss an employee, but does not have grounds for dismissal or wants to prevent going to court. The agreement has to be in writing and signed by both parties.

Its legal implications are as follows:
- The employment relationship ends on the date that is set in the agreement, without application of notice periods
- Usually the employer pays a severance payment (*Abfindung*), which is usually the reason why an employee agrees to such an agreement. This *Abfindung* is treated generously tax-wise, as it is tax-free up to a certain amount. Anything exceeding this amount is subject to a lower tax rate than the general salary.
- The employee will not get unemployment money if the last day of his employment is earlier than it would be under the notice periods. Unemployment money will only be paid as of

the first day after the notice period. Therefore if you don't have new employment, you should make sure that the Aufhebungsvertrag does not shorten your notice period. If your employer wants you to stop working immediately, he can give you paid leave until the end of the notice period.

• The employment agency (*Bundesagentur für Arbeit*), that takes care of unemployment benefit and finds employment for people does not pay unemployment benefit for the first three months if the employee terminates his employment. Therefore, in order to avoid this happening to the employee, the employee should never agree to an *Aufhebungsvertrag* (because an *Aufhebungsvertrag* implies that the employee has given in his notice, not that he has been dismissed!) Only if the employer issues a notice letter and the two parties then reach a mutual agreement is the Aufhebungsvertrag not considered to be proof that the employee gave in his notice.

I sincerely hope that you will never be dismissed, but if it ever happens, you should get a lawyer immediately. Also, note that if you want to contest a dismissal in court, you are required to do this within three weeks after receiving your notice letter, so don't waste any time as it can be crucial.

x) Reference letter (*Zeugnis*)

An employee's entitlement to a reference letter from his employer has already been mentioned. The employee is not only entitled to such a recommendation letter when the employment relationship has ended (*Endzeugnis*), but also when there are major changes during the employment relationship (for example a new boss, transfer to a new position or another department or a merger with another company). In such cases, the employee receives an intermediate report, Zwischenzeugnis.

The recommendation letter has to be in writing (email is not sufficient!) and needs to include at least facts about the duration of the employment relationship as well as the kind of work done. An employee has also the right to demand that the reference letter includes an assessment of his work and conduct during the employment relationship. Generally, the employee doesn't necessarily need to point out that the reference letter should include an assessment of his work, this is implied in the request for the reference letter.

The *Endzeugnis* should be handed over to the employee on his last day of employment at the latest. If it is handed over with delay and the employee can prove that this has caused him a loss of earnings (for example, he was not able to successfully apply for a new position without the reference letter), the employer has to pay compensatory damages.

Reference letters need to be truthful without hiding any true facts (even if they are negative), even though general wording should be favorable. Formulations in recommendation letters are often cause for lawsuits. There are a number of books and websites informing about allowed and forbidden formulations and their meanings.

d. Social and cultural aspects of the working environment

Of course a country's culture also influences the work life. Therefore cultural awareness is important and crucial for a successful employment relationship. If you work in Germany you will notice certain things you might find unusual or even rude, but just like in daily life, the transition to a different work culture is much easier if you familiarize yourself with the cultural peculiarities that await you.

As mentioned, the German culture is formal and calling one's boss by his first name is usually not something a German employee would dream of doing. When I worked in the US and my new boss came in and told me to just call him "Mike", I wasn't even sure if he was serious. It certainly took me a while to be comfortable with this.

However, many companies, mainly international ones or of American origin, have adopted the custom of people addressing each other on a first name basis. Sometimes, when superiors are involved, it doesn't work out. I once worked in the HR department of an international company in Germany, when we received an email from the Head of HR letting us know that he decided that all German HR employees should address each other by their first names. People tried to keep it up, but most of them just couldn't get used to addressing the Head of HR by his first name and slowly, but surely, they just reverted back to calling him "*Herr* ....".

In some companies, colleagues of the same age and level quickly and easily revert to first names but continue addressing their bosses the formal way. Interestingly, Germans are very capable of adjusting when they are with foreigners. People who wouldn't dream of calling other Germans by their first names, easily do so with Americans. One expat from the UK made the following observation while working in Germany: "It was also quite hierarchical, although this didn't really apply to foreigners. The German staff would happily use first names and 'du' with the foreigners but be stiffly formal with each other."

You should wait and see what the atmosphere is like in the company you work in. As you just read, most people probably won't have a problem if you ask them to call you by your first name, as they are aware it is handled differently in other countries. In my work, we are used to addressing our expats by the first names (except those who also have German as their native language). – Just don't always expect Germans to be comfortable with you addressing them by their first names, especially not in the work environment.

If you work in Germany, you should know that the communication style is very direct, even more so than in the US and definitely more than in England or in Asian countries. If you come from a country where people use indirect communication, you will probably discover that your German colleagues don't always get the gist of what you say, because they are used to people saying directly what they mean (not beating around the bush!). It is very hard to change the communication style you are used to, so advising you just to be more direct isn't very helpful. (However, when you have the feeling that your German colleagues never react to your requests, take a moment to remember that they are not acting like this because they are not helpful, but simply because they probably didn't even realize you made a request.

In those of my intercultural trainings where expats from countries with an indirect communication style are present, I stress this point again and again. Once I was a bit worried that it was too repetitive, but then a British colleague gave me feedback about the training and especially pointed out how helpful it was for him that the topic of indirect and direct communication had received such in-depth treatment.

Also, if a German disapproves of an idea or a concept or has a different opinion, he will say so frankly and openly (with varying degrees of politeness). If a German thinks it's not a good idea, he'll say "It's not a good idea". No frills, no hints, just the direct statement. Of course, this also applies to private conversations. If a German doesn't share your opinion, he will tell you straight out and he won't mind letting the conversation turn into a - factual - disagreement. Disagreeing on an opinion, whether it is about politics, religion or sports, isn't considered to be a negative development in Germany. It doesn't harm the friendship (unless the discussion gets too personal, of course) and it is not considered rude to voice a different opinion (again: if this is done in a factual and non-insulting way). Germans are comfortable with agreeing to disagree, if it's necessary.

In the work environment this could also mean that your supervisor or maybe even colleagues might just tell you straight out if they thought you weren't doing a very good job. This open way of criticism can cause immense cultural conflicts, especially if a person comes from a country where criticizing a person would lead to him losing face - meaning that he would suffer a loss of respect or reputation. In such a culture people take great care not to formulate a criticism in an offending or hurtful way. Take for example Japan. If a Japanese supervisor is not satisfied with the work of one of his employees, he would merely imply this to his employee in a very considerate and gentle manner. The employee would know exactly how to interprete this, but he wouldn't "lose face". Imagine the situation of a German supervisor having to make a performance evaluation for a Japanese employee and neither side is familiar with the culture of the other. The German supervisor will probably say something along the lines of "I liked your work in that area, but it needs improvement in that area."

This would sound reasonable to a German, but a Japanese person would feel terribly insulted and believe that he had failed completely.

If you come from the US, you might not see the issue that strongly, but you still might consider your German supervisor's statement too blunt. Germans usually don't use the 'sandwich approach' regarding criticism, so they don't wrap every negative statement in two layers of positive statements to soften the blow. They are generally not so generous with praise.

You will probably not be surprised to hear that in business conversations and at meetings, Germans get straight to the point. Small talk isn't considered necessary, even though managers now are becoming aware of the significance of small talk in an international environment. Therefore many of them are now actually learning how to indulge in small talk, as it normally does not come easy to Germans. For business in Germany, building up a relationship is not important. If you come from an Asian country, you are probably used to business conversations revolving around entirely non-business subjects until a relationship is established, which can take a while. If a German manager meets a potential business partner, he most likely won't inquire about the other person's children, home, family life or offer to show him around the city. He will get down to business immediately.

I already mentioned the importance of punctuality. This applies even more so to the work environment. If you have a job interview, never ever come late, not even a minute. In fact, try to be a bit early. If you happen to be late, have a really good excuse. The same goes for business meetings. If a meeting is set for 10 am, people will start to come to the room around 9.55 am. It is considered extremely rude to let others wait for you.

Many expats noted that Germans separated their work and private life very strongly. This also means that they take great care to separate their work and leisure time and not let it overlap. If an employee's work hours are from Monday to Friday, having a pressing deadline won't necessarily mean that the employee would be willing to sacrifice his valuable weekend to come into the office. Generally, people are unwilling to do overtime. If working hours are from 8 am – 5 pm, people will usually leave at 5 pm (this doesn't include upper management level). Again, this strongly depends on the company culture. I have worked in companies where doing overtime was considered a sign of your dedication, so people just stayed longer because it didn't look good if they went home on time. On the other hand, I have worked in companies where people literally dropped everything at 5 pm and the offices were empty about 10 minutes later.

You might be pleased to hear that although colleagues like to keep their work life and private life separate, they can also be very sociable, especially when someone has a birthday or leaves the company. In Germany, if it's your birthday, you are expected to give your colleagues a treat. It doesn't have to be anything elaborate, a glass of sparkling wine (*Sekt*) and/or a cake or some nibbly things are just fine. It is not a big affair, but it is certainly something that shouldn't be neglected. An American friend of mine was amazed at the importance of birthdays in Germany. In companies, departments usually have birthday lists so that no birthday is forgotten and colleagues will surely congratulate you. It's not seldom that you will receive a gift from the colleagues in your department and if a colleague celebrates his/her birthday, you will be ask to contribute to a birthday gift.

When you leave a company, it is customary to treat your colleagues to something, it is called *Ausstand*. Here again, you will receive a small farewell gift from them.

You will probably discover an institution that underlines the significance of a lunchtime meal to Germans: the *Kantine* (cafeteria). Many companies have a *Kantine* where their employees can have an inexpensive meal (some *Kantinen* are also open to other employees of surrounding companies, even though they usually don't get to benefit of the special prices). On the whole, *Kantinen* don't have a very good reputation, just like other places where food is prepared for masses of people. Actually, they differ a lot, I have eaten in really good *Kantinen* with almost restaurant-quality food, but also in awful places where you get unhealthy, heavy and badly-prepared food. Most *Kantinen* offer a choice of three warm meals (often with one vegetarian option) as well as a salad bar and a soup and some sandwiches. Employees usually go to the *Kantine* together, in small or larger groups. – If the company doesn't have a *Kantine*, there are often plenty of restaurants or take-away services nearby to provide hungry workers with a warm meal.

During your work life in Germany you might encounter further cultural differences. Generally, the same applies here as in daily life: different behavior isn't automatically bad behavior or meant in a rude way, and when in doubt – just ask.

e.   Volunteer, self-employed and freelance work

As mentioned before, getting a job in Germany is everything but easy, especially if you need a work permit. Therefore, it can be interesting for you to consider alternatives if you want to do some kind of work.

Volunteer work comes to mind, as it is fulfilling, does not require a work permit and is easier to find than a regular job. However, volunteer work doesn't have much of a tradition in Germany. With their tendency to rely on the state, Germans were never prone to engage in extensive volunteer work. As volunteer work also requires people to have a basic knowledge of the German language, the possibilities for expats are quite limited. I asked expats whether they did any volunteer work and most of them said they didn't, but a few of them planned to do something of that nature in the future. Robert Lederman gave a very fitting description of the volunteer-work-situation in Germany: "Tried to, but they don't seem to do that here." – Even if you find volunteer work, it is probably less interesting and challenging than a volunteer function in the United States, as it is more common for professional organizations to take over really responsible tasks and leave the supporting work to volunteers.

Still, there are means and ways of finding something. The most obvious and easiest way would be to join one of the international clubs. They always do charity work and often eagerly look for people to take over a volunteer function. There is something for everyone's taste there and you – usually – won't have the language problem as you will be moving in English-speaking circles.

If you want to work in a German environment and if your language skills are sufficient, you can, for example, ask the churches whether they need anyone or whether they know of an agency looking for volunteers. There are many large cities now where stores like Oxfam are always looking for volunteers to work behind the counter. The internet sadly doesn't offer much information yet. If you know any helpful websites, feel free to email me the links to hwolf@wolfintercultural.com.

Some American friends of mine work as journalists for American or international magazines on a freelance basis. If you have a profession (or background knowledge) that would allow you to work as a freelancer, this is an option you should definitely check out (if you freelance for a German employer, you should first find out whether you need to get a work permit first).

As a self-employed person you usually don't need a work permit (still, there are formalities to be adhered to, so make sure to inform yourself thoroughly first at the *Ausländeramt*, which is responsible for these matters), although some entry visas can include a prohibition to work at all in Germany. Be aware that everybody working on a self-employed basis usually needs to register a business (exceptions are some so-called "free professions, such as trainers, where you only need to notify the *Finanzamt* of your profession). This is done at the local *Gewerbeamt* (trade agency; in some smaller towns this can be a part of the *Bürgerbüro*). In turn, the *Finanzamt* (inland revenue office) will then contact you, as you will have to make special tax declarations. This is something that has to be taken seriously, so you should either have a good knowledge of German or get the help of someone who can assist you with all the official German documents that you will be confronted with as soon as you start your business. If you do decide to become self-employed, you will need to have lived in Germany for more than three months. Therefore, you will need to take your residence permit and your passport along to the *Gewerbeamt*. Generally, this is all you will need, but depending on the kind of work you want to do, you should phone beforehand and ask what documents you will need to bring.

VIII. The situation of the accompanying spouse

"For a person or family to remain in Germany, it is important that the spouse and/or children are happy. As a senior executive, life is made easy for me, but my wife is completely cut off from interaction, making settling difficult."

The situation of the accompanying spouse unfortunately hasn't in the past received the attention it deserved from the companies that sent their employees on international assignments, although now there are signs that things are slowly changing. Often, companies consider it sufficient to involve their assignee in the preparation of the assignment, without wasting much thought on the assignee's family. This can be due to indifference, unawareness of the difficulties an accompanying spouse faces, or lack of money or time. One expat manager I talked to shocked me with her reply to my question whether she included accompanying spouses in her work. She told me that it already quite annoyed her when assignees came to her with their questions or were seeking advice and she didn't want the additional burden of having to take care of the assignee's family as well. If you are an accompanying spouse and find this attitude unforgivable, I completely agree with you. I'm glad that now I work at a company where the assignee's spouse is fully included in the assignment process.

1. Getting information

Most of the spouses who filled out the questionnaire mentioned that they had not, or barely, been included in the preparations and the sharing of necessary information. What many companies still overlook is that if the accompanying spouse feels miserable during the stay abroad, it can endanger the whole assignment so that the company not only ends up with a disillusioned employee, but it has also invested a lot of money in a failed assignment. Therefore, the spouse should never be neglected. There are many time- and cost-efficient methods of helping the spouse to prepare for and adjust to the assignment. As mentioned before, I always told my assignees that their spouses were free to contact me with any questions. Sometimes, just the fact that they knew there was a person they could address with their questions and problems seemed to be sufficient. Useful books for accompanying spouses often don't cost a fortune, so a company should make that kind of investment and supply these spouses with the necessary literature. They will definitely appreciate the gesture! Whoever works in expat management should strongly consider one or several of these measures. The assignee has a contented spouse, and the company an assignee on a successful international assignment.

If you are an accompanying spouse and you haven't been in any way included in the company's preparations, just ask them for some information yourself. It won't always work out, especially if a company shows no interest in the situation of an expat spouse or if they simply don't have enough manpower for the handling of international assignments, but it's always worth a try. You will discover during your stay abroad that you will probably need to take more initiative in certain matters than ever before in your life. I know of companies where expat spouses have organized their own network, so if you feel left alone by your spouse's company, you should take the initiative and try this option. Maybe you will become a real trend setter in the circles of expat spouses!

Don't fail to acquire sufficient information about your new home country, its social networks and possible job opportunities on your own initiative either. The internet provides many interesting websites including networks or forums, especially for accompanying spouses.

2. Sacrifices that will need to be made

Generally, it won't be your initial wish to go abroad as an accompanying spouse. Your partner will be given the opportunity by his company to go abroad for a certain length of time and even if it sometimes turns out to be tough during the stay, it can also end up being a very rewarding and exciting experience. The main reason for you to go probably is to accommodate your spouse. You should therefore – if possible – make an informed decision and be aware of the sacrifices you will have to make.

If you are a working spouse, you should realize that an international move will have a major effect on your career. In most countries, including Germany, it is not easy for an accompanying spouse to get a job and a work permit. Find out in what way such an interruption may influence your career. If your work means a lot to you and you know that you can't do without it, or if a long pause will lead to a major career setback, you should seriously consider whether you want to give this up. If you do this just to please your spouse, chances are that you will not only end up being terribly frustrated, but there is a danger that you might also blame your spouse consciously or subconsciously for your situation. I know a woman who had a flourishing career in her home country and then gave it up to follow her husband to Germany. She wasn't, and still isn't, able to find employment here and she has now reached a point where she is seriously considering going back home, even without her husband. Needless to say, her career problems didn't help her marriage a lot.

Most people have a close-knit social network of family, friends and maybe clubs or other associations. If you move to a foreign country, this network unfortunately doesn't accompany you. Of course, you can easily keep in touch with those back home, but it is not the same. You won't be able to just drop in for a chat with your best friend on the spur of the moment or ask your parents whether they can mind your children for a few hours. I know several expat spouses with small children, who really suffer because they are not able to organize their daily lives in a more flexible way due to the difficulties of finding a babysitter at short notice or not having any family members close-by. One lady told me that she really missed not having her parents or parents-in-law around. After all, grandparents truly love their grandchildren and if they have time, are usually willing to guard their grandchildren for a while, giving the mother a little more freedom. If simple every-day issues like going to the doctor or grocery shopping become a matter of meticulous planning, you will sorely miss the support of family members.

It is also tough to keep up friendships over large distances. My parents moved approximately every five years and each time my mother had to leave friends behind and of course after every move it always took time to make new friends. This got more and more difficult, because the older she got, the more she realized that people already had their circle of close friends or that they were very set in their ways. If you are the 'new girl in town', you won't make friends immediately. My mother often mentioned that although she had enough casual friends (neighbors, women she met in language, painting or sports courses), she sometimes missed having a close friend, who she could just call if she wanted someone to do some window-shopping with or to accompany her to a museum etc.

If you move to a country without having a basic knowledge of the language, there is a danger of you losing some of your self-confidence when you discover that daily tasks become much more complicated and difficult, just because the people you have to deal with don't speak English and, in turn, don't understand you or your needs. Just the fact that you don't always know what it going on around you or you don't know how to articulate any need you might have, can result in you having a feeling of helplessness. An American friend of mine told me how much she was looking forward to going back to the US for a visit because everything would be less of a task. For example, she told me that watching TV would finally be relaxing and for a moment I wondered why she found watching TV in Germany not relaxing. Then she went on to tell me that in the US she would be able to understand everything on TV and so watching would not be such a challenge or a linguistic exercise, but just a pleasant pastime. I think this remark made it first clear to me of how difficult living in a country, in which a language is spoken that one is not familiar with, must be. Everything becomes a challenge. The impact of living in a different culture is just the same. You should realize that you lose the feeling of familiarity once you move to another country.

As you read on page 108, your driver's license might not be sufficient to drive in Germany, so it is possible that you will have to depend on public transport for a while. Whereas this is usually no problem in large cities or their outskirts, it can be a serious obstacle if you live in a very rural area, as public transport services are often unsatisfactory in such regions. If you end up living in a village where a bus only stops twice a day, you will become very isolated, not just because of language problems or a missing social network, but simply because you are not be able to get around. It is hard to build up a social network if you are stuck in your apartment and can't get anywhere.

During an international assignment, you might find yourself more dependent on your spouse than is to your liking. If you are not able to work, you have to rely on your spouse's income. If you don't know anybody, your spouse might be the only person you get to talk to, and in the expat community you will often experience that people acknowledge you simply as an appendage of your spouse – not as an individual in your own right. It will be a problem for you if you don't have a lot of opportunity for communication during the day, to discover that your spouse comes home after a long and exhausting day at work and just looks forward to a quiet, relaxing evening – preferably without conversation.

It is very frustrating not being able to let off steam after having an exasperating day - needing half an hour to buy a loaf of bread, getting on the wrong subway because you are not familiar with the public transport system, rushing home before the babysitter leaves. Then your spouse comes home and you just want to vent your frustration about your awful day and his reaction is that he has had a hard day as well and just wants to rest. In the worst case, your spouse won't be able to imagine what a battle daily life might be to you and consider your frustration unfounded.

Although, at the beginning, you might be very occupied with activities like searching for housing, redecorating and furnishing your new home, exploring your new surroundings and taking language lessons; after you have settled in, you realize that you have much more time on your hands than is to your liking, especially if you are not a working spouse. This can lead to you brooding too much and creating a feeling of emptiness, as you slowly realize that you have no challenging tasks to give you a feeling of accomplishment and satisfaction.

So, make sure that you are aware of the obstacles that you will be confronted with, when you make your decision to accompany your spouse abroad. Underestimating such challenges will only make your stay abroad unnecessarily difficult. However, you are not completely defenseless with regard to the problems you will encounter. Good preparation is just one of many excellent countermeasures against such problems.

3. Overcoming obstacles

In addition to the problems, previously mentioned, of finding a job in Germany, the aspect of the stay in Germany being only temporary should not be neglected. Companies seldom tend to recruit people who they will need to replace after a relatively short period. On the other hand, the current difficult job market situation has forced many companies to revert to time-limited employment contracts, so that finding a temporary job in the current situation might not be as difficult as it would have been several years ago.

Another issue is the question of degrees. A lawyer with a US degree cannot necessarily work as a lawyer in Germany. Many degrees acquired in a European country are recognized by countries within Europe, but this doesn't necessarily apply to all professions. You should definitely first check out whether your professional education and degree are acknowledged in Germany.

Pages 167 - 169 described the chances and possibilities for job searching in Germany and from that you understand that the chances at the moment are not too good. If you have a profession that you can conduct on a freelance basis, you are of course freeing a better situation to consider employment possibilities outside Germany; especially as a journalist.

Many expat spouses have made use of their situation to find completely new fields of work. Teaching English (or other languages) is always a popular option, but there is surely much more you can do if you just think about what makes you special. So, if you are resourceful and can take the initiative, don't consider your stay abroad a loss of your career but rather the beginning of a new – and maybe even more rewarding – career. A good example is a friend of mine, whose stays abroad prompted her to enter the field of intercultural training and as she had lived in several different countries for a while, she was very qualified for it. If you search the internet, you will find websites and networks of other expat spouses dealing with the issue of how to work abroad (see page 8 for some links).

Don't rely on your spouse's company to help you with the employment issue. It is a big exception for a company to be active in the job search for an expat's spouse. It is more common for companies to pay a spousal allowance, either as a lump sum or as a reimbursement up to a certain amount. This allowance is meant to at least help the spouse financially with the job search. But in the end, you will have to rely on yourself and once again be flexible, show initiative and resourcefulness.

If chances of finding work are relatively small, there are alternatives for doing something rewarding. Learning German should definitely be one of them. If you can dedicate more time to intensive learning and practicing, you will greatly enhance your German skills. A friend of mine, whose partner was considering an international assignment, told me that she might use that time abroad to get an international degree. This can be a financially challenging solution, of course, but if you can afford it, it might certainly be worth looking into to. Universities have more and more programs for international students, the best-known examples are the LL.M. degrees for lawyers or the MBA degree for business students, to mention but a couple. Depending on your background, education and interest, you have quite a good choice of interesting university courses. Check out the universities close to your new home or contact international academic exchange services.

Of course, you don't have to pursue an academic degree. You can take the opportunity of learning something you have always wanted to learn. I, myself, would like to have more spare time because there are so many things I want to learn or skills that I would like to improve – like languages or quilting, as profane as it may sound. I would also like to spend much more time writing. If you end up in a foreign country with no work possibilities, this may be your chance to finally acquire that new skill you never had time for.

If you had a hobby at home, don't just give it up after your move. Most hobbies are internationally compatible. Maybe you never had time to indulge in a hobby. So, take the opportunity now! Join a gym and go there regularly, develop your creative skills by starting to paint or do embroidery. Write the book you always wanted to write. Take a course in cookery and surprise your spouse with new culinary skills. It's also never too late to start learning to play a musical instrument. The possibilities are manifold and almost everybody has something that he/she has always wanted to do, but never had time for.

But beware – simply taking up a new hobby is great, but it cannot fill the void left by losing a career. So, it is important to find something that really gives you a feeling of accomplishment. Otherwise, you might have solved the time-filling problem, but you still might not have that feeling of satisfaction.

Also, make sure that you don't only do things that isolate you. As mentioned previously, you will experience the loss of a social network. Therefore, it is important to nurture the already existing network as well as to establish a new one as soon as possible. If you decide to take a new university degree, you can combine this with meeting other international students, who in turn, will surely be open to friendships as you are all in the same boat – away from home in a country where you don't know anybody. Ideally, you should start building-up your new network before you even come to Germany – e.g. getting in touch with international clubs in your future environment as well as with the spouses of your partner's colleagues, who are already abroad. Try the internet as well to find expats in your new home town. Moving to a place where you already know someone – even if just by email – can be very comforting. The larger your social circle is in Germany, the less you need to depend on your spouse being the only human contact you have.

Emails and the internet make it easy to stay in touch with friends and family left behind. Many expat families now build their own websites to inform their friends and relatives about their new life. Building up and maintaining your own website can be a good and useful task in itself. You can choose whether you want to present the more private side of expat life or offer professional information to any future expats. Internet messenger programs offer you the opportunity of chatting with friends and family in your home country. If both users have a webcam and a microphone, it is possible to see and hear each other. No expat should ignore the vast possibilities of the internet.

As mentioned before, making new contacts can become difficult if you are isolated due to insufficient transport options. Before you choose your new accommodation, you should select the area you want to live in very carefully and find out how good the public transport system is there. Never move in an area that is too out-of-the-way! If you are able to live close to other expats (in certain towns there are real expat communities), that will help you with the initial contact making (although with time be sure not to limit your social circle exclusively to other expats!). The right choice of accommodation is absolutely crucial, especially if you are not mobile.

By creating your own circle of friends and acquaintances as well as finding a meaningful new task or job, you hopefully won't have more spare time on your hands than you prefer. Nurturing contacts with friends back home can also take up a lot of time. However, don't rely solely on such options. As an accompanying spouse from Australia points out: "As a trailing spouse (and this is country-independent) you have a lot of time for introspection, so keep busy!"

Don't let people reduce you to the status of being your spouse's appendage. If they are only interested in the work your spouse does, mention your own activities and achievements. Don't see yourself as being just an accompanying spouse. The more effort you make to lead an independent life abroad, the easier things will be.

If your new life is one of fulfillment and you have the support of a social network, your outlook will be much brighter and you are on the best way to making the assignment a successful one. Hopefully, after your time in Germany you will return home realizing that in spite of all the obstacles, you managed to turn your life abroad into a rewarding and enjoyable experience. In any case, you will definitely return home with some new skills, whether it be international work experience, a university degree, a profound knowledge of how to prepare German dishes or the mastering of a new language.

IX. International children

If you have children, you shouldn't underestimate the effects an international move will have on them. When I was a child, we moved approximately every four years and even though – apart from one move – we moved within the same country, I was devastated every time I was told that we would be moving again. If you consider the additional insecurities and worries an international move involves, you can imagine how upsetting such a move can be for a child.

Depending on the age of the child, it's reactions to a move abroad will differ. A toddler/small child, whose interaction takes place mainly within the family, will be more flexible, more curious and more willing to make new friends whereas a teenager, who has a close circle of friends and enjoys spending time with them, or finds social recognition among his/her peers extremely important and who might even have a boy-/girlfriend for the first time, will find his/her life much more disturbed by a move abroad. However, you can do a lot to make the international experience a happy and rewarding one for your child.

The most important thing is to keep your child informed about the moving process. Just as you like to know as much as possible about your new home country and what will await you there, your child will be just as eager for information. This is understandable, as it is a well-known fact that people fear the unknown. So, include your child in the preparations for the move as much as possible and let it take part in your research work about your new home country – depending on the age. If your child is internet-savvy, you can let it search for all kind of information regarding Germany, so it feels involved in the process and at the same time gets an impression of what to expect. There are also many websites with forums for expats and expat children, so you can get acquainted with people in the destination country before your move.

Whenever possible, give your child the impression that the impending move is something positive. If a child constantly hears its parents talking of how difficult everything will be in the new home country, it will find it hard to look forward to the move. Also, don't expect your child to be enthused right from the beginning and above all, take its concerns seriously. If your child tells you that it is worried about losing his/her friends and might not be able to make new friends, it won't be comforted if you answer with "Oh, you'll be fine, don't worry." As you yourself will have your own worries regarding the move, just imagine how you would feel if nobody takes you seriously. It might help to establish strategies that can alleviate your child's concerns – e.g. exchange email addresses and phone numbers with your child's friends, so that it will be easy for your child to keep in touch with all his/her friends after the move and at the same time find out what your surroundings in the new country will be like and what ways there are to make new friends there. As mentioned in the previous chapter, making a website with information about your new life in the destination country can be a good way of keeping busy and staying in touch with those back home at the same time, so get your child involved in this new and exciting project. Even though you will probably be extremely busy before and after the move, make sure you spend enough with him/her and listen to any anxieties or worries it might have.

If you have small children, the issue might not necessarily be to prepare the child for the move, but to make sure that you have a good social and support network in the host country. Find out as much as you can about kindergartens, playgroups, babysitter availability and mothers' groups as soon as possible. International clubs often have special groups for mothers with small children, so they are a good place to start. Of course, once again, the internet will provide you with a wealth of information on this subject.

If you come to Germany with children, sooner or later you will have to decide whether your child should visit an international school or a German school. A friend of mine who has lived in Germany for several years now, found this a very hard decision to make. Sending your child to a German school has the advantage that he/she will get to know German children and will constantly hear the German language as well as learn more about the German culture, which can facilitate life in Germany considerably. It is also worth considering that German children (future friends!) are not as likely to move away after a few years as expat children might do.

The international school of course is a valuable option if you move to Germany with older children who don't have a basic knowledge of the German language. It is impossible to follow lessons in German without having any knowledge of the language at all, so in that case you might not have any choice but to send your child to an international school. The international environment and atmosphere at such a school are also highly beneficial to a child, even more so if your future plans anticipate your moving to various different countries in the following years. As mentioned above, the problem for children at an international school is that most of them are expat children, meaning that friendships only last for a limited period, only until they have to move away again after a few years. On the other hand, your child is in a similar situation as the other expat children, which can also be helpful. One other point that speaks for international schools is their high educational level. Unfortunately, Germany's education system has deteriorated in the last few years. Once reputed for its good quality, it is now infamous for lessons being canceled for insignificant reasons and the lack of a more competitive education. Even German parents who can afford it are considering putting their children in private and international schools to make sure that they get a good education. A fact that has to be mentioned is that international schools are very expensive and not all companies provide financial support for the education of expat children. Some companies provide no financial aid at all, others take it into consideration only if the local school system isn't considered adequate. Unless the company you or your spouse work for chips in with the costs or you are able to finance school funds yourself, you might find sending your child to an international school too expensive.

As you can see, it's not easy to make the right decision regarding the school system. Apart from the financial aspect, there are also certain other factors to be considered - the child's age (it's easier for small children to learn another language) and school grades as well as the duration of your stay in Germany. Another aspect not to be neglected is the fact that your child will be confronted with two different cultures – the culture at school and the culture at (an expat) home. Children who are exposed to different cultures during adolescence are called Third Culture Kids (TCKs). This situation does not only have a positive effect on children, but it can also have the consequence that children feel lost between two cultures and don't know where they belong.

To ensure that such a significant move abroad has a positive effect/impact on the development of your child, it's very important for you to collect as much information about your new future location as you can. Here are a few links where you can find further information about moving with children:

- www.travelwithyourkids.com
- www.tckworld.com
- www.expatbabies.com

X. In a nutshell

I hope by reading this book, you have learned a little about Germany and the Germans as well as how to get along in this new environment. Of course there are always unchangeable factors that will influence your stay here, but you can do a lot to make your life in Germany a pleasant and positive experience. Here are the basic issues of the book in a nutshell:

- As soon as you know you are moving to Germany, get as much information about expat life and about Germany in general as you can.
- Make sure all administrative matters are settled (health insurance, immigration, translations and copies of diplomas if you plan to look for a job, etc.).
- If you are an accompanying spouse, make sure your partner's company includes you in all preparation stages of the assignment.
- Determine the area for your new home with regard to transportation access, expat communities, schools or shopping facilities.
- Don't let negative first impressions rule your entire picture of Germany.
- Don't be determined not to like Germany or your expat situation even before you move there – because then you will definitely end up not liking it and what good would that do?
- Get a computer and internet access as soon as possible.
- Prepare for culture shock
- Remember that "different" is not necessarily bad.
- If you experience a culture-related custom/reaction/behavior, try to determine the reason for it in order to understand cultural differences better.
- Learn German.
- Build up mixed social circles, don't mingle solely with expats and definitely avoid the company of expats, who only acknowledge the negative aspects of their situation.
- Be open-minded and tolerant.
- Take initiative.
- Keep busy.
- Do some sightseeing.

- Try local specialties and pastimes.
- Inform yourself about good doctors and emergency services so that you won't have to search for information during a medical crisis.
- Learn even more German.
- If you want to work in Germany, inform yourself of the requirements and opportunities.
- If you can't work, find a rewarding substitute/activity.
- Be determined to make your stay a unique experience.

Good luck and enjoy your stay in Germany!

XI. Closing Words from Expats in Germany

You read about German culture, the intricacies of daily life, the importance of learning the language and how to get on in the work environment. I hope it's encouraging for you now to know that whereas you will find some things are very different to what you are used to, they can be dealt with and, who knows, you might even learn to appreciate some of them. Living in another country is a wonderful and special experience and I sincerely hope that you will view your stay in Germany in this sense. I asked the expats in my questionnaires if they had a special memory of Germany that they would like to share. So, to give you a first impression of what you might come across during your stay in Germany, please read about some of the special experiences other expats had while they were here.

A young expat from the UK mentioned the following: "Heated political debates over beer or outside in the vineyards are happy memories. Boat trips down the Rhine, singing Karneval songs and shouting for sweets from the procession floats, looking yet again and a plate of Spargel and wondering why Germans get so excited about this vegetable..."

Bonnie Barski, an American who has lived in Germany for many years, remembers how family life developed here: "Getting married at the Standesamt [registry office] in Schlüchtern and the party in the Ad Agency afterwards. Over the years we've had many memorable experiences, of course – having a baby and raising him, career experiences. There are so many."

Sarah Happel from the US did something that probably not even many Germans get to do: "Paragliding over Neuschwanstein Castle in Bavaria."

Alice Waldron, another expat from the UK, who has lived in Germany for several years now, values the central position of Germany: "The Weihnachtsmarkt is nice and traditional. – It is exciting being in the middle of Europe and having so many possibilities for travel and enough holiday to be able to do it!"

The travel is something Maureen Chase also treasures, especially as so many beautiful areas are close to where she now lives: "Our Sunday drives to the Rhine and Lahn Rivers. (...) I enjoy the freedom and the beauty around me. Those are carefree days, like I am on vacation."

An expat who came here as an accompanying spouse from Australia, distinguishes between the extraordinary and the German daily life: "Exciting: probably going down the baby slope on a snowboard for the first time without falling! Typical: going to beer gardens and eating Obatzda in summer, catching the U-Bahn, cobblestone streets."

Ron Dixon, from Zambia, appreciates the German efficiency: "I really enjoy the fact that most things run very well and smoothly and that everything is so tidy and clean. The Germans still maintain very high standards which are disappearing around the world."

These are just a few of the experiences expats so kindly shared with me. But these examples illustrate how everyone cherishes a different special memory and that there are many interesting experiences to be made – the sports, the traveling, a different kind of daily life, watching your children grow up in another country, enjoying life in a different cultural environment – you will surely find something to enjoy and appreciate.

All expats stated that their stay in Germany had been very fruitful and all of them would not mind going abroad again. So let's end this book with a few more reflecting closing words from 'our' expats, who have accompanied you throughout this book:

"I like Germany a lot. I have invested time and effort in learning German and about Germany. It isn't though an easy country for foreigners to live in and it's difficult to really integrate."

"[My personal and professional results of my stay in

Germany were] some fantastic friends, a network of colleagues I know I'll work with in the future, very happy memories and a more international and tolerant outlook on the world. – My friends say I've been Germanised!"

"Tell your expats that the Germans actually have a lot of humor and are really friendly!"

"When we first lived in Germany, I was often homesick for the States. But after living in Florida so long, I'm really enjoying being here again. I think also, just the little things like McDonald's or Kentucky Fried Chicken and being able to get the American foods at the grocery stores, greatly reduces the things you miss."

"We made and still make our living in Germany. It seems to be where you start out is where you build up your life's financial basis. Personally (...) one changes so much through adapting to the other culture. One doesn't want to miss the new culture then. Both cultures give you different enjoyment levels."

"I think Germany, particularly Frankfurt is a great place for foreigners because people here are used to outsiders and the infrastructure is here to allow for a pleasant quality of life. I look forward to learning more about the culture and of the language so I may enjoy my experience even more. And the Germans are a lot friendlier than they are made out to be!"

Index

A

B

C

D

E

F

G

H

I

K

L

M

N

P

Q

R

S

T

U

V

W

Z

Made in the USA
San Bernardino, CA
17 October 2018